Editor: Ellen Wilton, Former School Librarian

Project Manager/Photo Editor: Eva Soos Szoke, *Parent, Class of 2007*

Graphic Design/Production: J. Ennis Kirkland, *Alumni Parent, Class of 1998, 2001*

Manufactured in China by C&C Offset Printing Co., Ltd.

(Printed on acid free paper)

ISBN-13

978-0-9790849-1-1

ISBN-10

0-9790849-1-1

Library of Congress Control Number: 2007920756

Publisher: Woodside Priory School, 302 Portola Road, Portola Valley, CA 94028

(650) 851-8221   www.woodsidepriory.com

Published by Woodside Priory School

2007

On October 18, 2006, Fr. Egon celebrated his 90th birthday. Exactly 51 years earlier he crossed the Bay Bridge for the first time in his life, searching for a home for a small group of exiled Benedictine monks.
—Photo by Eva Soos Szoke

Dear Friends of Woodside Priory,

It is a pleasure for me to write some words of introduction to this book in which Father Egon recounts the story of the founding a half-century ago of King Saint Stephen's Monastery and Woodside Priory School. You will undoubtedly notice that there is a recurring refrain throughout Father Egon's text which points to the presence and the power of God's mysterious Providence at work in every phase of the Priory's early years of development.

How else can we hope to explain the undisputable fact that without Communist oppression in post World War II Hungary, Woodside Priory and School would never have come into existence? We wonder how it is possible that a political movement halfway around the world more than half a century ago brought to birth in California what Father Egon repeatedly calls "An American Miracle." Is it by pure chance, mere coincidence, the vicissitudes of history, or random happenings? Others may be satisfied with one or the other of those explanations. We are not. As our late Pope John Paul II once remarked: "In the designs of Providence there are no mere coincidences."

We, as men and women of faith, believe that God in His inscrutable Providence and unspeakable love utilizes all manner of persons, events and things to create ever-new miracles for His glory and our benefit. The human elements and instruments are, to be sure, always imperfect. But this, too, is a part of the miracle. Almighty God has the power to bring good out of evil and order out of chaos.

The mysterious ways by which such "miracles" take place is never fully understandable by human reasoning alone. But when viewed with the eyes of faith, we develop a profound awe and deep gratitude for God's presence and Providence in our lives and in the lives of the institutions which form a very part of who we are as persons.

I can personally attest to this mysterious unfolding of the Providence of God in my own life, having entered the Benedictines here at the Priory in 1968. I am grateful to God and to my Benedictine confreres here at the Priory for providing me with my initial formation in the monastic life, the opportunity for theological and professional education, and most of all, the nearly forty years of monastic fraternity that I have been blessed to share.

The story you are about to read is primarily a testimony of gratitude to God for His blessings on Woodside Priory and School over the past fifty years. It is also a grateful testimony to those instruments through which God chose to accomplish His work: Father Egon himself, the other monks who assisted in the Priory's founding and early years, and the many other Benedictines who have served here during the past fifty years, whether from Saint Martin's Archabbey in Pannonhalma, Saint Anselm Abbey in Manchester, New Hampshire, or from other Benedictine communities. In a special way, we thank and commend the confreres who presently serve here in the Priory community: Father Martin Mager, Father Egon Javor, Father Pius Horvath, Father Maurus Nemeth, and Brother Edward Englund. We pray, too, for those confreres who have died. May the Lord reward them generously for their faithful work and prayer on behalf of the Priory community.

And finally, through Father Egon's phenomenal ability to remember and recount the critical involvement of the Priory's early friends and benefactors, we, the Benedictines, express our profound gratitude to the many men and women who from the very outset have generously supported the Priory by sharing their time, talents and treasures with such unfailing fidelity. This story makes it clearly evident to all that the providential design of God for the Priory would never have been realized in such an abundant measure without the assistance of our many friends, colleagues and benefactors who, in a very real sense, were co-founders of Woodside Priory and School. Again, in the name of all the Benedictines, thank you and may God bless you and your families abundantly.

Once again, I thank and commend Father Egon for his pivotal role in the founding and building up of the Priory as we gratefully commemorate fifty years of Benedictine work and prayer, faith and perseverance, service and scholarship here at Woodside Priory and School.

In closing, let us pray in the words of Saint Benedict, "May we prefer nothing whatever to Christ, and may He lead us all together to life everlasting." (Rule of Saint Benedict 72:11).

Abbot Matthew Leavy, O.S.B.

Saint Anselm Abbey

Manchester, New Hampshire

FOREWORD

ON NOVEMBER 11, 1956 — the Feast of St. Martin, the patron saint of the Archabbey of Pannonhalma, Hungary — Fr. Egon Javor, O.S.B., celebrated Mass in an improvised chapel in a small old ranch house in Portola Valley, California. This marked the end of a long search for a home for a group of displaced monks and the beginning of the Woodside Priory and School.

The following is the account of the establishment of the monastery and school from the notes of the founder, Fr. Egon, in his own words as he wrote it. It has been my privilege to assist Fr. Egon in recording his memories and acknowledging many of the persons who helped him in those early days.

Ellen Wilton

Librarian, Woodside Priory School,

1975-79, 1983-1994

Fr. Benignus Barat   *Fr. Achilles Horvath*   *Fr. Emod Brunner*

Fr. Christopher Hites   *Fr. Stanley Jaki*   *Fr. Leopold Hoffer*   *Fr. Egon Javor*

CHAPTER I

THE SUMMER OF DECISION

IN 1955 THERE WERE SEVEN BENEDICTINE FATHERS from St. Martin Archabbey, Pannonhalma, in Hungary, living in exile in the United States: Fr. Emod Brunner, Fr. Christopher Hites, Fr. Benignus Barat, Fr. Egon Javor, Fr. Leopold Hoffer, Fr. Stanley Jaki, and Fr. Achilles Horvath. Six lived in the same geographical area and came together occasionally to keep in contact and discuss their plans for the future.

The Hungarian Benedictines had their first reunion in the United States during the summer of 1951, at St. Ann's Hungarian parish in Pittsburgh, where Fr. Leopold Hoffer was assistant priest at that time. Fr. Brunner, as senior, was responsible for carrying out the desires of the archabbot of Pannonhalma. Fr. Archabbot Pal Sarkozy urged the fathers, in his occasional letters and messages, to make a serious attempt to establish community life. However, Fr. Brunner was cautious. He was convinced that any untimely move toward a Hungarian Benedictine foundation would necessarily end in failure, and his colleagues accepted his prudent advice at this time. He proposed the policy of waiting, learning the language, and getting better acquainted with the American way of life. While they waited, all earned their living by teaching or by pastoral work. Some also studied for degrees in American universities.

In 1955, Fr. Brunner taught a course in theology at the downtown campus of Fordham University in New York City. He lived in a neighborhood Franciscan parish. Fr. Christopher and Fr. Benignus were the guests of St. Mary's Abbey in Newark, N.J. Fr. Christopher was teaching Latin at St. Benedict's prep school, and Fr. Benignus was the chaplain of the local Hungarian population, celebrating Mass for them in Hungarian in the abbey church. Fr. Egon enjoyed the hospitality of St. Mary's Priory in Morristown, N.J. (later to become St. Mary's Abbey). He was assigned to the faculty of Theology, teaching the Benedictine clerics and occasionally substituted in the monastery's high school, conducting classes for the students of Delbarton School.

Fr. Leopold was working for his doctor's degree in biology at Fordham and received room and board in a Franciscan parish. Fr. Stanley also studied at Fordham for his doctorate in nuclear physics. He lodged with the Sacred Heart sisters at their Manhattanville College campus at Purchase, N.Y. Fr. Achilles was farther away at St. John's Abbey, Collegeville, Minnesota, where he taught dogmatic theology at the seminary.

In 1955 the majority of the group was ready for a change. Three of them, Frs. Brunner, Egon, and Leopold were naturalized citizens. All had mastered the English language (only Fr. Egon never lost his heavy Hungarian accent). They understood the mentalities of the American people, and they were acquainted with the customs and life styles of the country. Fr. Brunner still preferred waiting in dispersion, but others grew impatient with his procrastinating attitude and thought the time ripe for coming together somewhere in their own home and finding the field of their common activity.

They had the following options:

1. To continue in dispersion, postponing any attempt for community life.

2. To join their exiled Hungarian Benedictine confreres in Sao Paulo, Brazil, who

    had established their own priory and opened a school.

3. To try to start a foundation of the Hungarian Benedictines here in the United States.

Against the first, life in dispersion, they had serious arguments. The most important among these were the responsibility toward their mother abbey in Hungary and the obvious dangers of the prolonged individual life. Their desire to reunite in monastic community was growing with the passing years. Although they were well accepted and sincerely enjoyed the hospitality of the country, and were busy in their studies or work, a certain feeling of loneliness followed them everywhere. The common past, the sweetness of the mother tongue, the memories of bygone days, and the tragic history of communist-occupied Hungary and of the archabbey bound them together; they naturally felt at ease in each others' company. In spite of the well-known burdens and frictions of life in common, the sense of loneliness made them impatient with the idea of prolonged dispersion.

The sense of duty and responsibility toward their mother abbey was also a moving power. They felt deeply grateful for their spiritual and intellectual foundation received at Pannonhalma. In spite of distance and emigration, they still belonged there. Almighty God helped them to reach freedom. It would be selfish to pursue individual goals now while their mother abbey struggled under oppression and in poverty. They must do something fruitful for the benefit of the abbey they had left.

In 1955 it was obvious they could find a successful future in the United States remaining separated, going on their own as free individuals. They could serve the needs of the Church, the country and their fellow men, as guests of American monasteries, as teachers in schools and universities, or as priests ministering in the pastoral work of parishes. They could even help their confreres in Hungary with their earnings. However they would remain lonely individuals and at the end would find a lonely death. On the other hand, with a serious attempt they could come together and establish their own home. The fruit of their common work and prayer could become a new Benedictine foundation and the continuation of their old archabbey in the new world.

The prolonged life in dispersion harbored dangers and liabilities for monks, of which the fathers were fully cognizant. The regularity of their structured monastic life already had been disrupted years earlier at the end of World War II. The Russian occupation of their homeland in 1945, and the nationalization of their properties and schools in 1948, changed their lives in Hungary. After they left their country and reached the free part of Europe, a long waiting period followed before they became eligible for immigration to the United States. Even in this country those who found homes in Benedictine monasteries were considered and treated as guests and enjoyed certain privileges and freedom. Those who lived in parishes were more free. Although they informed Fr. Brunner from time to time about their life, work, and finances, essentially they depended on their own decisions, earned their own income, and provided for their own necessities for several years. Such freedom carries certain dangers from a monastic point of view. Experience has proved in many cases how difficult it is for those who enjoyed freedom and independence for long periods outside the walls of the monastery to return to the regularity of community life, into the yoke of obedience, of stability, and to the duties of choir and assigned work. The temptation to make a free lifestyle permanent sometimes becomes overwhelming.

For these and other practical reasons, the Hungarian fathers decided against the first option: to remain in dispersion.

The second option required a new migration, to leave the United States and join their fellow Hungarian Benedictines in Sao Paulo, Brazil.

Since 1928, Hungarian Benedictines had been taking care of the spiritual needs of the many Hungarian-speaking Catholics who settled in that promising great South American country. Four were there during World War II, and this number was swelling with the arrival of others who left Hungary after the war. They had their own house and parish in one of the suburbs of the fast growing metropolis of Sao Paulo. Also they published a Hungarian weekly newspaper. In 1952 they succeeded in establishing their own monastery, the St. Gerard Priory, and opened their own school, the Collegio Santo Americano.

The idea of joining their confreres was not without its attractions and was highly promoted by one of the monks of Sao Paulo, Fr. Englebert Sarlos. During the summer of 1955, he took a group of Brazilian students from their newly established school on a tour to the United States and spent a few days in New York. One warm evening he gave first-hand information about their bold endeavor to the Hungarian fathers gathered around him.

Fr. Englebert was a classmate of Fr. Christopher and Fr. Benignus in the novitiate. He served as a military chaplain of the Hungarian army, and at the end of the war he was captured and spent four years in a prison camp in Russia. There he learned perfect Russian. His captors, knowing him from the prison camp, were after this talented young priest to make him their agent in Hungary after he was released. Fr. Egon helped him escape from Hungary in 1948, and his fortunate arrival in Brazil followed one year later. He spoke several languages, was an excellent mathematician and a good educator with a great knack for discipline. Eventually he became the headmaster of their school in Sao Paulo and a professor at the university.

Fr. Englebert spoke with great enthusiasm about their life and successful work in Sao Paulo. He informed his attentive audience how they studied the school system and education laws of the state of Sao Paulo, and how they perfected their Portuguese and passed examinations to become qualified, accredited teachers in Brazil. They rented buildings of the Catholic University in the heart of the metropolis and opened their school with classes from grammar school to college preparatory included. He described vividly the joy of teaching in their own school but was amusingly naive about many aspects of a new foundation, especially the finances. He did not hide the difficulties involved, but he did stress the advantages. The fathers in Brazil were on their own, had security in the future, and were involved in creative activity in their flourishing new school. The success of their beginning filled them with satisfaction and new ambitions. The group in New York, still in dispersion, heard with admiration the story of their Brazilian confreres.

Fr. Englebert mentioned that they were in need of more teachers in their school. As his confreres had not yet started their own community life in this country, instead of waiting for an uncertain future, should they join them in their established monastery in Sao Paolo? The idea was not without its attractions. It would end the separation and uncertainty and would offer life in their own community among those whom they knew from the old country, from the mother abbey. After the years of exile and loneliness they would have a home and could continue their teaching activity in their own school. They could also serve the spiritual needs of the Hungarian Catholic immigrants in Brazil in their mother tongue.

After the visit of Fr. Englebert, the fathers held long discussions about a move to Brazil, and slowly they saw the long and frightening shadows of the sunny and attractive elements. Brazil was a far-away country with a hot and humid, tropical climate. The language of the country was Portuguese and the temperament of the people, Latin. To teach in a school in Brazil, a diploma or teacher's credential was required from a local university. Joining their confreres in Brazil meant another move, learning a new language, a new national mentality, and starting a new life. It would mean more years of learning before teaching or being able to do some useful, intelligent work and throwing away the fruits of all the fine experiences acquired in this Anglo-Saxon environment. It was hard enough to go through all that once, years ago, when they first arrived in the United States. It would be twice as hard the second time. Strangely, the visit of Fr. Englebert, instead of promoting migration to Brazil increased the desire, in the hearts of the fathers, to establish a new foundation of their own here in this country.

The final impetus to embrace the third option was given by the visit of Fr. Gerard Bekes at the end of August of the same summer. Fr. Bekes was Procurator of the Hungarian Benedictine Congregation and professor of dogmatic theology at the Benedictine Pontifical University, the San Anselmo, in Rome. Because of the Iron Curtain, communication was difficult between the free Western World and Hungary. Consequently, the archabbot of Pannonhalma designated Fr. Bekes a "superior major" and invested him with the authority and rights of the archabbot over the Hungarian Benedictines living outside Hungary. Those members of the congregation who had the good fortune to leave the country reported to him, and he gave direction to individual monks to remain in Europe or to migrate to the United States or Brazil. Fr. Bekes arrived in August 1955, from Brazil, where he had visited the new foundation. He gave a complete and objective picture of it to his confreres, who welcomed him in New York. This was his first visit to the United States, and during his stay he had long conversations with all of his subjects and had the opportunity to stay in some abbeys, getting information from American abbots as well. He evaluated the situation and saw the dangers in the lives of his monks living in dispersion. He found the hopes for a successful new foundation, of such a small foreign group without money, very slim. Still he thought that those monks who could manage their individual lives well in this new world could do as well or perhaps better in a common project. Therefore he confirmed the order of the archabbot of Pannonhalma: the fathers must find a solution for community life in the United States within one year, or failing to do so, must join their Benedictine confreres in Brazil.

All accepted this decision of Fr. Bekes. It reflected the opinion of the group that they must try first, using the coming school year for exploration of the possibilities and make a serious attempt to obtain a permanent home in the United States. The political instability and uncertain conditions in South America, including the country of Brazil at the time, justified this resolution. It was more desirable that the Hungarian Benedictines have a foothold on both of the American continents, not only in South America, but also in the North, especially on the solid soil of the United States. Following the advice of Fr. Bekes, the majority of the fathers remained in their present positions, while Fr. Christopher and Fr. Egon were charged with the work of exploration.

CHAPTER II

PRELIMINARY PLANS

UNDER NORMAL CIRCUMSTANCES the opening of a new monastic house is not a complicated task. A mother abbey, ready to send out a group of monks, comes to an agreement with a bishop of a diocese concerning the location of the new religious house and the type of work the newcomers intend to do. The mother abbey provides all the necessities for the beginning and bears an obligation to support the new foundation with monks and provisions as needed.

In the case of the Hungarian Benedictines the solution was not so easy. They were on their own. The mother abbey in Hungary, struggling under the suffocating oppression of a communist state, was unable to give support of any kind. They could not go to a benevolent bishop, in the location of their choice, with an attractive, well-prepared plan of a monastery, school, retreat house, or seminary, according to their wishes, and offer their services to enrich the spiritual or educational life of a diocese, because they did not have any capital. They felt completely at the mercy of Divine Providence concerning the questions of: a) where to find a suitable place, b) what type of work to do, and c) how to start without funds.

These three questions formed a vicious circle. Without funds it was unrealistic to select a location. The location would determine the right type of work for the monks, by which they would earn their living. A generous donation of property could settle the question of location. An invitation to teach in a high school or seminary, or to take over a retreat house would determine the type of work. Any donor could attach special conditions to a gift, or any bishop could explain his demands, according to the special needs of his diocese. Only by offering useful services could they move any bishop to give permission to settle under his jurisdiction; only by the filling of a special need of a locality could they find financial support. This was obvious at the beginning of their search.

If they had capital, they most likely would select a populated area with a good climate, surrounded with colleges or universities, and would establish there a monastery and live the Benedictine life. Their work would be giving conferences in ecclesiastical and liturgical topics, conducting retreats for small groups, helping in pastoral ministry at parishes or accepting academic jobs in higher education. The future development of their monastery would be in the hands of the Lord. However, without the necessary funds, such a solution could only remain a dream. They had to face the hard facts: they were only seven, of foreign origin, and with the urgency of becoming settled within a short year. Therefore their task was unusually difficult.

While keeping all of these problems in mind, some ideas about their possibilities were slowly crystallizing. Their search had to be concentrated around areas with the following conditions: a) where priests were needed and seven able priests would represent a positive asset in the pastoral work of a diocese, b) where there was a shortage of Catholic schools and teachers, and where the Benedictine name and fame in the field of education might be wanted, and c) where the Benedictine order was not yet present. In such a place the implantation of the Benedictines would carry a sense of the new, especially where the inhabitants knew something of the liturgical, cultural, and historic values of this old monastic order.

A subjective consideration of the Hungarian group was the problem of climate. Coming from a country where they were accustomed to four distinct seasons with a dry winter and summer, they all suffered considerably under the humidity of the eastern United States. They were middle aged, and to fulfill their daily duties, they opted for a mild and dry climate.

The cultural environment of the location was also important to them. They brought a valuable treasure of the Benedictine scholarly and cultural past to the new world, and naturally they preferred to settle among people who could recognize and appreciate the Benedictine spiritual and educational tradition they were able to offer. Consequently, not only their future occupation, but also the cultural level of the location was important to the fathers as they formulated their plans. The Hungarian congregation was acknowledged as a scholarly unit of the Benedictine Order. The Archabbey of Pannonhalma had its own department of philosophy and theology for the training of the younger members to become priests and teachers. Several Hungarian Benedictines were professors at state universities in Hungary and abroad. Some always studied in different universities of Europe. Their schools, the Benedictine gymnasiums, enjoyed high prestige and excellent reputations in educational circles. Their graduates were welcomed in the leading universities of Europe. The members of the Hungarian Benedictine Congregation had the most doctoral degrees among all of the Benedictines at the time of World War II.

The Benedictines who reached the United States from Hungary were well equipped intellectually. Of the original seven who established the Woodside Priory, three had doctor's degrees in Sacred Theology, one in Philosophy, one in Biology, one in Physics, and one held an American teacher's credential. They spoke several languages, and some studied music and art. The doctoral thesis of Fr. Stanley, about the church, was a classic at the time, known and used in the theological departments of universities and seminaries. Fr. Egon edited seven medieval manuscript missals in Hungary, and his work is mentioned among the sources of Andreas Jungmann's "Missarum Sollemnia," (First Edition) the best edition about the history of the Mass. During his early years in the United States he translated the Sunday Missal into Hungarian to serve the Hungarian Catholics abroad. (When the monks later came together in California, five had background and experience in teaching at American universities and seminaries and two in high schools. Consequently, their choice of work was also determined by their intellectual preparations and experiences.)

The third question, "how" followed the previous questions of "where and what?" How could they bring the religious group together and create a home for them without money? Intellectually they were equipped to fulfill priestly or scholarly duties, but they lacked the necessary capital to establish their own monastery.

As refugees they arrived in the United States with only bare necessities. Some of them crossed the Atlantic with the help of the International Refugee Organization. In the beginning of their American life, they used their meager incomes to supply adequate clothing for winter and summer and the most essential books for learning and for teaching. Those who continued to study at universities had to pay tuition, while those who had pastoral work were obliged to buy cars to fulfill their duties. All of them had to spend to help others. Requests from relatives, friends, priests, former students, or new refugees, all in greater need, arrived in abundance to the fortunate ones who reached the United States. Therefore, the fathers could not save much. In Benedictine monasteries they received hospitality, full room and board, but a very small salary for their work, and they had to provide for their personal necessities. Therefore, some of the group took better paying positions outside monasteries with the idea of saving for their common future. As long as they lived in dispersion no "community chest" was established among them, and each managed his own financial problems. Serious saving by the group occurred only when their future in the San Francisco Archdiocese was assured.

The fact that they lived in the United States mitigated the serious problem of how to finance the new foundation. The generosity of Americans, of American Catholics, especially after World War II, was fabulous. The valuable donations of the National Catholic Welfare Conference arrived in Hungary immediately after the war and continued as long as the communist regime tolerated this capitalistic aid to a socialist country. The Hungarian fathers had ample opportunity to observe in monasteries, schools, and parishes, how the gifts of the people supported Catholic institutions, built churches, and founded schools. Consequently, they cherished the hope that, if they did good and useful work, they would also reap some share of this great generosity of the American people.

In 1952, Fr. Egon worked at St. Mary's Abbey in Morristown, New Jersey.

CHAPTER III

POSSIBILITIES IN THE MIDDLE WEST

BEFORE THE DECISION IN THE SUMMER OF 1955, the fathers were on the alert to find benevolent bishops and call their attention to the existence of this Hungarian Benedictine group.

Fr. Leopold, who for years was assistant at St. Ann's Hungarian parish in Pittsburgh, came in contact at some priestly gathering with Fr. Joseph Annabring, who was born in the United States of Hungarian parents. When Fr. Annabring became bishop of Superior, Wisconsin in 1954, Fr. Leopold wrote to him offering the services of the Hungarian fathers. The bishop was gracious in his answer and was willing to take them into his small diocese, which at the time numbered only seventy priests. He was not eager to establish schools and could not offer special financial aid. However, he expressed his hope that the fathers would be supported by the farmers of that large agricultural diocese in any endeavor they might start.

Fr. Egon, serving in a parish on Sundays in New Jersey, while working at St. Mary's Abbey in Morristown, assisted at the first Mass of a young priest from California. Later he talked to this father and learned from him of the scarcity of priests in the large diocese of Monterey-Fresno. The growing population required priests for the future spiritual and educational needs of that sunny state. He corresponded with Bishop Aloysius T. Willinger of Fresno, who was a religious himself, a member of the Redemptorist Order. Bishop Willinger was willing to open the doors of his diocese, but he would have to scatter the fathers for some years in his parishes, far from each other, before further plans could develop. Continued dispersion in the far West was not attractive to those who were looking for life in common.

With the unanticipated visit of Fr. Gerard Bekes during the summer of 1955, Fr. Brunner suddenly became very active. He had a suspicion that the unexpected arrival of Fr. Gerard from Brazil would involve the whole group's immediate transfer to the newly established priory in Sao Paulo, and he was the least inclined to go there. Partly to prevent such an order and partly to have something to demonstrate to Fr. Gerard that this group also had possibilities for a permanent home in the United States, he made a quick trip to St. John's Abbey in Minnesota and to Benet Lake Priory in Wisconsin. Fr. Brunner started his life in the new world at St. John's and taught there for several years before he obtained a teaching position at Fordham, closer to the other members of the group. Consequently, he had good connections at St. John's Abbey and could assure the moral and perhaps even the financial support of that abbey for a Hungarian Benedictine foundation.

Benet Lake in Wisconsin had a very active prior at that time, the future Abbot, Fr. Richard Felix, a man of extreme ability with many ideas and friends. He was interested in the Hungarian fathers. In 1950 he made an attempt to lure them under his jurisdiction with an offer of property in Pennsylvania. That would have required the transfer of vows, which the Hungarian group declined to accept.

Fr. Richard Felix always had a place in mind for a new foundation. He took Fr. Brunner to Detroit, Michigan, without delay, introduced him in the chancery office of the diocese, and secured a rather vague, verbal permission for the Hungarian Benedictines to settle in the Archdiocese of Detroit. To assure some influential local help, Fr. Brunner was introduced to the famous radio-preacher of the Roosevelt era, Fr. Charles E. Coughlin, pastor of the Little Flower Shrine in Royal Oak, a suburb of Detroit. Fr. Coughlin was short of teachers in his parochial high school, and Fr. Brunner offered him the assistance of the Hungarian Benedictines. Returning to New York, he gave an account of his trip to his confreres and showed them the pictures of some property for sale in Northern Michigan suggested by Fr. Felix as a possible location for the new foundation. He presented the results of his trip to Fr. Bekes, also.

New assignments for two of the monks resulted from Fr. Brunner's trip. In September, Fr. Christopher went to assist Fr. Coughlin in his school and parish in Royal Oak, and Fr. Egon obtained one year of leave to explore further possibilities.

In September 1955, Fr. Christopher and Fr. Egon duly inspected the property in Northern Michigan with the expert guidance of a real estate agent. They drove fifty miles north from Detroit, through flat agricultural land, colorless in spite of the approach of autumn. The two hundred acres for sale contained neglected farm and pastureland with a small green belt of forest. The four insignificant buildings, scattered over the land, were neither large enough nor suitable for monastery, chapel, or school purposes without extensive alterations or additional construction. The location was too far from residential areas, and the small village in the vicinity served only as a shopping center for the farmers, offering no cultural background for a high school. The opinion of the local real estate expert was that students could be recruited to the school from Detroit, and only small fees could be charged from boarding students in that particular part of Michigan. It was enough to see the place, evaluate the possibilities, and make some calculations to find it unsuitable for a resident school. With good conscience the two decided against this choice. Neither Fr. Brunner nor Fr. Richard was too happy upon receiving this information from Fr. Christopher.

Shortly thereafter Fr. Brunner received a letter from the vice chancellor of Edward Cardinal Mooney, of Detroit, informing him that the cardinal accepted with favor the idea of a Benedictine foundation, but had reservations about the location. Fr. Brunner instructed Fr. Christopher to keep in contact with the chancery office.

After exploring Fr. Brunner's plan in Michigan, Fr. Egon drove farther west, to South Bend, Indiana. In this flourishing town, next to the University of Notre Dame, there were many inhabitants of Hungarian descent. There were two active Hungarian parishes. The pastor of St. Elizabeth of Hungary Parish was an American-born Hungarian, Msgr. John Szabo, a well-respected priest, a leading personality of Hungarians in America, and the president of the Hungarian Catholic League. Fr. Egon enjoyed his hospitality and discussed with him the case of the Hungarian Benedictine fathers. Msgr. Szabo was enthusiastic about the possibility of Hungarian Benedictines taking root in the vicinity of South Bend. In those days there was no private high school for boys in that area, although there was a very good private school for girls. He was an active man, and a good deed followed his encouraging words. Bishop Leo Aloysius Pursley, auxiliary of Bishop Knoll from Fort Wayne, was in town. Msgr. Szabo took Fr. Egon to him for a private audience, and the bishop invited him to a confirmation where a large group of priests were present. The bishop and priests were all friendly and welcomed the idea of a Benedictine high school.

Fr. Egon spent two weeks in South Bend and the area. He visited Notre Dame University, also schools, convents, properties, parishes, and priests around Notre Dame. He soon knew that he had to take the search elsewhere. In this flat rural area there was only one outstanding towering institution: Notre Dame University. Nothing else counted. Mighty Notre Dame absorbed all the interest and support of the Catholics. Concerning potential donors he found another obstacle. Although Saint Meinrad Archabbey was far away in the southern part of Indiana, the whole state was somehow St. Meinrad's territory. The majority of the secular clergy graduated from St. Meinrad's Seminary and their allegiance, naturally, bound them to that abbey. It would be an intrusion on the part of another Benedictine group to start a new foundation near South Bend.

Putting Superior, Detroit, and South Bend in reserve, Fr. Egon set out toward the far West.

Chapter IV

California

SINCE HIS EARLIER CORRESPONDENCE with Bishop Willinger in Fresno, Fr. Egon never had forgotten California. He took out maps, read books, studied statistics, especially those in the heavy volume of the Catholic Directory, and learned more and more about the Golden State. Not only was he impressed, but slowly he saw all of the preliminary conditions for a foundation come into focus on the Pacific coast; the growing population of the Catholic Church necessarily demanded more priests, more schools, and more teachers. He felt that the Hungarian fathers had good opportunities in the Los Angeles or San Francisco Archdioceses, and he determined to explore these far away places into which the Benedictine Order never before had penetrated. Individual Benedictines worked in the San Diego diocese, there were two Benedictine parishes in Los Angeles, and some Benedictine nuns taught in parochial schools in Southern California, but no abbey or priory was yet established in the state.

As Fr. Egon planned to make Los Angeles his first destination, he turned west after leaving Indiana. En route he visited Chicago, the two Hungarian parishes in the city, and one in South Chicago. He also went to the Cistercian abbey of Okachee, Wisconsin, where the father abbot and some monks were Hungarians, and where the Hungarian Cistercian refugee fathers found a home before they settled in their own abbey in Irving, Texas. He spent a day at the famous Boys' Town of

Fr. Flanagan in Omaha, Nebraska, where there was always a shortage of priests and two or three could find positions at any time. Then he turned toward the Wild West.

The lure to the West was promoted by Monsignor Stephen Kerner, with whom Fr. Egon was corresponding. This diocesan priest was well known and respected in Budapest, where he was the spiritual director of the theologians at the university during the years when Fr. Egon studied there. He escaped from Hungary after the communists took over and later came to Los Angeles. At the time of his death he was a member of the seminary at San Diego. When Fr. Egon located him, this highly educated priest, who held a doctor's degree in sacred theology from Gregorian University in Rome, lived in a parish at Compton and instructed religion in a Catholic high school.

Msgr. Kerner's letters to Fr. Egon were filled with enthusiasm. Francis Cardinal McIntyre was responding to the needs of his archdiocese in Los Angeles with a tremendous educational program. He was opening new schools and recruiting teachers from religious orders. He accepted not only Msgr. Kerner, but gave jobs to many other refugee priests in his schools. Msgr. Kerner felt sure that the Benedictine fathers could come to a satisfactory agreement with Cardinal McIntyre and urged Fr. Egon to visit California.

The prediction of Msgr. Kerner proved to be correct, but for another group of Hungarians. A few years later Cardinal McIntyre gave a home to the Hungarian Norbertine fathers in exile. Some of them were obliged to teach in the diocesan high schools, but they obtained his permission to establish their monastery and open their own high school, St. Michael's in El Toro.

Fr. Egon knew that teaching in diocesan Catholic high schools would not look too attractive to his colleagues. However, such an opportunity could bring their group together to begin their own community life and could serve as a temporary solution. He was truly amazed by the example of Msgr. Kerner, who — in his seventies at the time and with very broken and seldom correct English— fulfilled his duties with praiseworthy zeal and to the satisfaction of the superintendent of the Catholic schools. The younger Hungarian Benedictine fathers could do the same, thought Fr. Egon.

Fr. Egon expressed his gratitude to Msgr. Kerner for all of his encouragement when as prior he invited the monsignor to preach the annual retreat to the monks in the Woodside Priory during Christmas vacation in 1958, the second year of the school's existence. The monsignor admired the primitive poverty of the young monastery and school, and had the satisfaction not only of preaching a retreat, but knowing he was instrumental in bringing the Hungarian Benedictines to California.

Providence led the Benedictines elsewhere, and they never presented their application to Cardinal McIntyre in Los Angeles. Before going to Los Angeles, Fr. Egon wanted to see the city of St. Francis by the Golden Gate. He also intended to visit the DePotteres in Palo Alto, whose children he had baptized previously in the East.

While driving west, appreciating the excellent roads, he felt the immensity of the United States and the beauty of nature in the landscape. He stopped at Denver, crossed the Rockies of Colorado, visited the Mormon Tabernacle in Salt Lake City, drove through the desert of the Great Salt Lake and Nevada, and traveled onward toward the Sierra. Although he enjoyed the trip, his heart was heavy with the importance of his mission. He did not want to be simply a tourist who has to return to the East after a long sightseeing tour of the United States. He must find a home for his refugee group. Therefore, he prayed hard, while holding the steering wheel and following the setting sun, that Almighty God may guide and lead him to the promised land. On his 39th birthday (October 18, 1955) he crossed the Bay Bridge when the sun was setting over the fabulous hills of San Francisco. From the first instant he felt at home in the Bay Area and never wanted to go any farther. Before continuing to Los Angeles, he decided to stay and explore the chances of the Hungarian Benedictines in San Francisco.

He started his work with concentrated precision. He must have an address and phone number to present in the chancery office, and he must learn quickly about the leading personalities of the archdiocese, especially of the chancery office. He asked the hospitality of the Franciscan fathers in their centrally located St. Boniface house on Golden Gate Avenue. Fr. Harold, the guardian, received Fr. Egon with kindness because he was a Benedictine, a member of the order that donated to St. Francis his beloved "portiuncula," the little church of St. Maria degli Angeli, outside of Assisi. As customary in religious houses, he got his cell, his place in the community refectory, and helped daily in St. Boniface church or elsewhere saying Masses, according to the needs of his hosts. His stay turned out to be longer than he expected.

There was a small Hungarian colony in San Francisco, and Fr. Joseph Jaszovszky was the chaplain of the Hungarian Catholics. Fr. Jaszovszky wrote articles in the Hungarian Catholic's Sunday newspaper, presenting quite a splendid picture of the importance of his work and of his people in the far West. The reality was more modest, as Fr. Egon found when he introduced himself to the priest at the Sacred Heart Parish. The jovial looking, not too tall, corpulent father received him with reserved friendliness. As it turned out, he was an alumnus of the Hungarian Benedictine fathers in the gymnasium of Esztergom as a minor seminarian and had many memories about his Benedictine teachers. When Fr. Egon explained the reason for his presence in San Francisco and his desire to settle the Benedictines in the archdiocese, Fr. Jaszovszky turned negative. He gave a depressing picture about such a possibility, telling Fr. Egon frankly that he would be knocking on the wrong door and should continue his trip to Los Angeles, where he would find better chances of success. Fr. Jaszovszky cited several examples demonstrating the attitude of the chancery office: secular priests, Hungarians and others, were refused admission to the archdiocese. The archbishop turned down the Hungarian Cistercian fathers, a larger group of more than twenty priests with money, only five years ago; how could the Hungarian Benedictines, a small group without money, expect any better reception?

Such talk certainly was not encouraging, but not alien to Fr. Egon's ears. One Benedictine father told him, in New Jersey, the story of the German Benedictines from Maria Laach, who tried so hard for years during World War II and did not succeed with a foundation in the United States.

How could the Hungarians have any hope? Fr. Egon knew of one of their group, Fr. Damasus Winzen, who later started a monastery in Elmira, New York. Fr. Abbot Patrick O'Brian had warned him in the same way when he took leave in Morristown. "It is no use to go to San Francisco," he said, "Mitty will kick you out." Such was the reputation of Archbishop John J. Mitty: he did not like religious orders.

Fr. Egon did not lose heart. He had come this far, and he was determined to test his chances in San Francisco. From the long conversation with Fr. Jaszovszky he learned one important and useful fact: the key person in the chancery office was the chancellor, Msgr. Leo Maher.

Fr. Jaszovszky maintained this cool attitude until the Benedictine fathers had made their final agreement with Archbishop Mitty. He never invited Fr. Egon to say Mass, preach a sermon, or hear confessions in Hungarian, never introduced him to any of his Hungarian Catholics. One year later, he asked Fr. Egon to be the Hungarian speaker at his 25th anniversary. At this time there was no other priest in San Francisco who could qualify for this honor.

From the Franciscan fathers Fr. Egon received the same information about the chancery office. They told him there was no use in visiting the auxiliary bishops or spending any effort on other priests. The archbishop's ears were open mostly to the words and suggestion of his chancellor. After due preparation, Fr. Egon went to the chancery office of the archdiocese.

In those days the chancery office on Church Street, in the block of old Mission Dolores and the Mission Basilica, was still a new and modern building. The chancellor was free to receive Fr. Egon without delay. Instead of an old and morose monsignor, to his surprise, Fr. Egon met a young, well-built, smiling and kind priest in the chancellor's office, Monsignor Leo T. Maher. He was very friendly and open. The Benedictine father felt at ease when he introduced himself and told of his group and his mission here. Msgr. Maher studied the credentials Fr. Egon presented to him and asked many questions about his background and that of the Hungarian Benedictines now in the United States. The monsignor showed a genuine interest. When other visitors were announced, instead of dismissing Fr. Egon, he took him to the office of the superintendent of the schools of the archdiocese, Msgr. James N. Brown. He was also a friendly, communicative young man with inquisitive eyes and fast speech. Msgr. Brown had spent some years in Washington, D.C. at the Catholic University and had studied with quite a few Benedictine priests. He remembered especially Fr. Stephen Findley, O.S.B., whom Fr. Egon knew very well as the headmaster of Delbarton School in Morristown. Discovering this lucky coincidence the conversation became very easy. Monsignor drew a picture of the secondary education in the archdiocese and expressed his appreciation for the Benedictine schools in the United States.

Fr. Egon had no intention at this first visit of seeing Archbishop Mitty. He only wanted to introduce himself, to let them officially know that a Hungarian Benedictine was looking around in this archdiocese and make his stay legal from the first moment. It is not a good introduction when they hear rumors in the chancery office about a priest moving around without presenting his credentials. Therefore, it was to his great surprise that when he returned to Monsignor Maher's office from Msgr. Brown's, the chancellor simply told him that his Excellency wished to see him immediately. Without time to protest, the door was opened to his Excellency's office, and Fr. Egon stood before the mighty and awesome Archbishop John J. Mitty.

The archbishop was very fair and correct and not at all the intimidating or overawing personage of his reputation. A long conversation followed the introduction, first with personal questions about the war, the Russian occupation, and the effects of communism in Hungary. Luckily, Fr. Egon mentioned his military chaplaincy with the Hungarian army in Russia during the war. This proved to be a good introduction. Archbishop Mitty was also a military chaplain during World War I and loved the topic. Instead of asking questions, he became talkative, telling about his past, how many churches and schools he had built since becoming archbishop of San Francisco, and the general situation in his diocese. At the end of this audience he dismissed Fr. Egon with instructions to stay with the Franciscan fathers, look around freely in the city and vicinity, and return to the chancery office after a few days.

At his second visit Fr. Egon again saw the two monsignors and the archbishop. He took courage from their friendly interest and presented the idea of his staying here longer, working in some of the parishes, and forgetting Los Angeles if the archdiocese would consider taking in the

Hungarian Benedictines. To his surprise, they accepted this plan without hesitation and promised to find a centrally located parish where he could live and work until further agreement could be reached. At this time Msgr. Brown concentrated his questions on secondary education: what would be the aspirations of the Hungarian Benedictines concerning a high school? Msgr. Maher was more interested in learning the willingness of the Benedictines to provide pastoral ministry, giving help to the parishes. Archbishop Mitty's questions also were more specific about the group.

On this occasion Fr. Egon was more specific and explained the value of the work of the Benedictines for centuries in his native country. They were missionaries of Hungary and had about eighty abbeys before the wars with the Turks in the 16th century. They had a strong influence on the religious and intellectual life of Hungary with their schools. The archabbot of his monastery was "abbas nullilus" with his own diocese and a member of the Hungarian senate, as were all the other bishops. He did not fail to mention that Rome regarded with esteem the members of his abbey, elevating two of the monks to the rank of cardinal within the span of the last half century: Kolos Cardinal Vaszary and Justinian Cardinal Seredy. Archbishop Mitty knew the famous canonist Cardinal Seredy and his involvement in the preparation of the Codex Juris Canonici in cooperation with Cardinal Gasparri. This link also helped Fr. Egon's cause.

As everything was developing much better than he ever dared to expect, Fr. Egon returned to his quarters at the Franciscans with high hopes and genuine good cheer. He expected the call from the chancery office within a few days. To his surprise and disappointment he had to wait for this call for almost a month.

By staying in San Francisco, he had a definite address and could resume his correspondence with his confreres. Fr. Brunner eased his anxiety in a letter during the long weeks he waited for the call from the chancery office. Fr. Brunner suspected that the archbishop, if he was serious in his consideration to keep the Hungarian Benedictines in his archdiocese, would not be satisfied to see the credentials only of Fr. Egon, but must check the background of the entire group and would most likely be in contact with the apostolic delegate, Amelito Cicognani, in Washington, D.C. That process naturally would need more time. The longer waiting period, consequently, must be taken as a good omen.

Fr. Egon felt embarrassed before the good Franciscan fathers; he originally sought their hospitality for only a few days. They were very understanding and kind, even welcomed his stay. Somehow they were short of priests to fulfill the many pastoral demands, and Fr. Egon happily accepted the different assignments to say Mass or to assist at High Masses or funerals in various parishes or convents each morning. He learned a good deal about the Catholic life of the city by doing so. He found the company of the Franciscan fathers very enlightening and useful also. As a rule, religious houses in the downtown area are good places for ecclesiastical gossip, and he gathered much worthwhile and practical information about the priests, pastors, and religious houses of the city by listening attentively. By accident he made his most important social contact for the future Priory by remembering a conversation with one of the Franciscan fathers at St. Boniface. He certainly got the most authentic lessons about Fr. Junipero Serra and the early California missions during his stay. He met one elderly Franciscan father who could recollect vividly the happenings during the 1906 earthquake.

Fr. Egon used this waiting period to become acquainted with the city and Bay Area. He systematically visited the churches, the Catholic high schools for boys and girls, and the headquarters of the leading religious orders, first in San Francisco and later in the suburbs.

He spent hours at Stanford University, the University of California at Berkeley, and Santa Clara University, studying the styles of the architecture, the richness of the libraries, the statistics of enrollment, and the subject fields they offered. He ventured farther southward to Monterey and Carmel, making a pilgrimage to the tomb of Fr. Junipero Serra. Another trip took him to the wine country in the Valley of the Moon and in the Napa Valley. This last place was so similar in climate and in the beauty of the countryside to his native Hungary, that he had a desire to start a monastery there. He took time to see a ballet in the opera house and attend some musical events in the city. Even the Grand National Rodeo and Horseshow at the Cow Palace were on his list of activities. By observing the audience as well as the performance he became informed and up to date in local affairs and was able to be a part of conversations with local people at later times. For the same reason he carefully read the daily papers of San Francisco. Thus the long waiting period, although taxing his patience, was very useful for Fr. Egon in learning the Catholic and cultural life of San Francisco and the peninsula.

Finally, toward the end of November, he was summoned to the chancery office. Msgr. Maher informed him officially that the archdiocese wanted to offer hospitality to the refugee Hungarian fathers and welcomed them, the first Benedictines in this archdiocese. His Excellency, the archbishop, designated the area around Modesto, in the central valley, where there were no other religious houses as yet, and Fr. Egon should continue his search for a foundation in that region. He continued that his Excellency would use him without delay at St. Joseph Parish in Cupertino in the Santa Clara Valley. The pastor there had an urgent need of an assistant. His Excellency, the archbishop, received him, told him the same, without specifying the Modesto area, and encouraged him to look around freely for opportunities and to return to him whenever he had a specific plan.

Fr. Egon left the chancery office with satisfaction. The archdiocese did not reject the group of Hungarian Benedictines but accepted them. He had a foothold, a place to stay and to work in one of the parishes of the archdiocese. The future was open for a Benedictine foundation here. He realized clearly from the instructions given by Msgr. Maher, that the first interest of the diocese was to have a religious order in the central valley, Benedictine or any other, it did not matter. There was a necessity to help the parishes on Sundays and on many other occasions with Masses and confessions, also with any type of pastoral services when the pastors were in need, sick, wanted to go on vacation, or could not fulfill their duties alone. In the mind of Msgr. Maher, a school was not a prime consideration, but the pastoral ministry of a religious order was. On the other hand, the instructions of his Excellency were much more broad. They gave him the freedom to research and an invitation to return to him with specific plans. Consequently, he took all this as a good overture, knowing the rest must depend, as Fr. Brunner wrote him, on "his wisdom and skill." He took leave from the Franciscan fathers, expressing his gratitude for their hospitality, and found his way to St. Joseph's Parish in Cupertino.

CHAPTER V

CUPERTINO

WITH A MAP TO GUIDE HIM, Fr. Egon found the St. Joseph Church and rectory on old Highway 9, the Saratoga-Sunnyvale Road, which at that time was a narrow winding road lined with beautiful trees between lavish fruit orchards. The church was new, having been dedicated just one year earlier. It was the last church dedicated by Archbishop Mitty; although he lived in good health for many more years, he delegated such functions to his auxiliaries. The patron saint of the church, appropriately, was St. Joseph of Cupertino, famous for his levitations and obedience. The rectory was old, not too large, but comfortable enough for two priests and a housekeeper. It also had a guest room.

Fr. Philip Ryan was the pastor. He arrived from Ireland in 1927 with the last group of imported priests to the archdiocese. From that time until the turmoil following Vatican II, the archdiocese had sufficient vocations from within its own boundaries. Fr. Ryan (later monsignor and pastor at St. Thomas Apostle Church in San Francisco and St. Monica's also) was all alone in his fast growing parish and certainly needed an assistant.

Fr. Egon rang the bell of the rectory after visiting our Lord in the church and asking his blessings for his future work in this parish. The secretary admitted him and announced him to the pastor. There was no mail delivery in Cupertino at that time, and Fr. Ryan had not checked his mail at the post office, so he had no idea he was getting an assistant. He did not even have a room for

Fr. Egon because two priests conducting a mission in his parish from the archdiocesan mission band were his guests at that time. But he was most gracious and friendly. He phoned his neighbor in Saratoga, Fr. Gerald Geary, and directed Fr. Egon to that parish to spend the night and to return the next day.

Fr. Ryan had a soft but very definite Irish brogue, and Fr. Egon had a strong Hungarian accent, which made conversation hard to understand. This first encounter scared both men quite a lot. The following Sunday was the first occasion on which Fr. Egon had to preach a sermon in English. To his great dismay he discovered Fr. Ryan in the back of the church listening. Fr. Ryan was most eager to find out whether the parishioners would be able to understand this Hungarian Benedictine with his strange accent. Fr. Egon passed the test because Fr. Ryan assured him that his sermon was understandable, and he had no further worries.

Fr. Ryan really needed an assistant. The large new church could seat more than five hundred people. There was only one Mass on weekday mornings, but five on Sundays, and all well attended. Because the majority of the parishioners were young, there were many baptisms, weddings, and some funerals. Sodalities for men and women were fashionable in those days and regular parts of the parish life. One evening a week was reserved for the devotion of Mary, the Perpetual Help. According to the proper seasons of the liturgy, other evenings were reserved for the stations of the cross, novenas, convert classes, and pre-marital instruction. Confessions were regular and heavy in those days. There was plenty of work for two priests. On Saturdays the parish overflowed with children who came for catechetical instruction. Baptisms, usually more than one at a time, took place after Sunday Masses. The weekends were also inundated with weddings. In addition to regular activities, a drive was in process to collect money for the building of a parish school.

The entire Santa Clara Valley was changing. The beautiful, large orchards were sold for housing developments. The old roads enlarged for growing traffic, and new schools were built. Hospitals, office buildings and shopping centers grew like mushrooms during the year that Fr. Egon spent in the parish.

He soon felt at home here and discovered the advantages of its location. He praised Divine Providence for directing him to this place, through the orders of the archbishop.

The location was quite good, about fifty miles south of San Francisco. Although it was some distance from the main artery, Highway 101, it still was only about a one-hour drive to the city of St. Francis. Cupertino is located on the southern end of the Peninsula. It is very close to San Jose, which was just at the point of awakening and growing into a city, close to Santa Clara, and on the western edge of the beautiful Santa Clara Valley. The oldest school in California, the Jesuits' Santa Clara University, was only a few miles away. High schools for boys and girls, Bellarmine, Notre Dame, Sacred Heart, and Saint Francis, were all close. New parishes were being cut out from old larger ones because of the growing population. Santa Clara county was the fastest growing place in the entire United States at the time. Hewlett Packard Company and Lockheed Corporation moved in to employ about 15,000 new workers who needed homes, churches, and schools. Thus, Fr. Egon, in a flourishing young parish, saw from the beginning this growing and changing California.

The pastor under whom he served was an ideal man and a good priest who enjoyed the challenges of his apostolic mission. Fr. Ryan kept a cheerful and kind attitude in all of his work and was very friendly with his parishioners. He divided the responsibilities with Fr. Egon justly. Because of the fund drive, the construction of the parochial school, debt on the church, and the many demands of his ever-growing number of parishioners, he was under some pressure and appreciated the help of a reliable assistant. He was able to enjoy some recreation, especially golf. It also created a smooth and workable solution for Fr. Egon, who took the parish responsibilities seriously when Fr. Ryan went out, and enabled him to go out for his special research when Fr. Ryan was present. They never failed in understanding and fulfilling their duties during the ten months Fr. Egon spent there as an assistant.

Fr. Ryan was very hospitable. Priests were always guests at his table, especially on weekends and Sundays. This way Fr. Egon became acquainted with many of the priests and monsignors of the archdiocese, learning the mentality and customs of the local secular clergy, listening to their joys and complaints, and some of the inner politics of the fast developing archdiocese. Msgr. Maher, the chancellor, and his successor Msgr. Thomas Bowe, were also among the dinner guests. These friendly encounters with the secular clergy, especially with the chancellor, around cocktails and dinner, were important contacts for him and eased his way to the chancery.

The information that Fr. Ryan supplied to them about Fr. Egon's work and reliability was also of value.

An unexpected advantage, and a very useful one in learning about California society, was the fund raising campaign that was going on at that time for the construction of the parish school. Fr. Egon was able to follow the procedure of this from the beginning to end. He saw the cross section of a parish financially, how the parents reacted to the drive, how much they pledged, and how they were willing to sacrifice for the education of their children in a Catholic elementary school. He studied the location of different streets, the value of homes in the various sections of the parish, the social division of the parishioners according to jobs and income, and the willingness of the men to take an active part in the drive. This study was very useful to him later when he selected the site of the Benedictine school and calculated the support of the population.

As the parish school was the purpose of the drive, he was able to follow the architectural plans and the actual construction during his stay in Cupertino. The architect and the contractor were often at the site. Fr. Egon could see the blueprints and follow the building program from ground-breaking to the dedication of the completed school. (By coincidence, the contractor was the brother of Bishop Pursley, whom he previously met in South Bend, Indiana.) He learned about building materials, costs of construction and of later upkeep, light fixtures in classrooms, and problems of heating. He talked daily to the workers and organized union members, and he evaluated their mentality and their working habits.

He also witnessed the organizing and running of a parish festival on the grounds that was very successful and brought in considerable income for the school. His work brought him in contact with the parishioners and their families. Some became and remained his faithful friends, offering help in the form of advice or financial support to him later when the Priory was established.

One more advantage of the time in Cupertino for Fr. Egon was that he met a Jesuit father, Clement Conway, who came to the parish every weekend to help with confessions and Masses. On Saturday evenings and Sunday afternoons, they had long conversations. Fr. Conway was teaching in Bellarmine High School in San Jose, but because he studied in the Los Angeles area and taught in various Jesuit schools previously, he had broad experience in the field of Catholic education in California. Fr. Egon learned from him how the Jesuit schools operated, what the tuition and board fees were, of the life in the dormitories on school days and weekends, the types of students who attend private schools in the Bay Area, their problems, and the reaction of parents to discipline in the schools. He received much other useful and practical information, not the least of which was how to cooperate with and how to remain independent from the educational department of the archdiocese.

The parish work soon became routine. By meeting people, taking part in conversations and doing the parish duties, his English, which had not developed well within the walls of the monastery where silence dominated the greater part of the day's order, improved quite well. By conducting the weekly devotion to Mary, the Perpetual Help, he learned the problems and difficulties of the local people. In this devotion many parishioners deposited written notes and placed them in a special box next to the picture of Mary, the Perpetual Help, and the priest read these aloud during the devotion. It was enlightening to see what kind of requests and problems were presented weekly to the Mother of God for solution. The long hours of confessions revealed much about the intellectual and spiritual level of those who confessed and gave insight to their knowledge of the Catholic religion. Fr. Egon enjoyed the convert classes and baptized eighteen adults as a result of this work.

Following the instructions of the chancellor, Fr. Egon visited the town of Modesto and its vicinity in the Central Valley a few times. The countryside was interesting: rich agricultural land with miles of beautifully cultivated fields and orchards. Walnut and almond orchards were planted with irrigation ditches carrying water to the trees. He never saw such a method in the old country. The grapevines grew old as small trees, so different from the vineyards of Europe. Large and comfortable houses were everywhere in the midst of the ranches, surrounded with cars, trucks, and agricultural equipment. Fr. Egon visited priests and schools to get information on the religious and cultural conditions. Although most of the population was Catholic—many of Portuguese origins—and church-going and supportive, they did not show much interest in schools or in higher education. Their sons and daughters attended the public school without too much interest or effort in learning, drove their cars and trucks, or rode their horses, happily preparing for the life of farmers. His best source of information about the Modesto area was his own pastor, Fr. Ryan, who had spent years in Manteca and knew the country and mentality of the people there. Fr. Egon soon decided that Modesto was not a suitable location; it was not populated enough to support a private boarding school. The school the Benedictine fathers intended to establish and the type of education they were able to offer must be close to San Francisco.

Fr. Egon started to study real estate in order to learn the correct process in starting a school. He did this not in a formal way, but just by going around with real estate agents and listening to their talk. Soon he met the representatives of many agencies who were eager to show him all kinds of properties and estates, even schools for sale. They came to pick him up—drove him around, according to his free time for viewing property—and brought him back to the parish. These agents only knew that he came from the East, represented a group of the old and prestigious Benedictine order, who intended to settle and start a monastery and school in this archdiocese, and it was his duty to find a good location for their purposes. That this group of Benedictines was only seven penniless refugee priests, they did not know. They carried on grand talk, praising everything in California, furnishing information on their local parishes and schools, dropping names of big benefactors and people interested in good education. Their stories of local history provided a good and inexpensive education for a newcomer. Fr. Egon was eager to listen and learned a lot; he hadn't known anything about real estate before. Now he learned to check the sunshine, the wind, the water, the soil conditions for septic purposes, the townships that prefer horses to churches or schools, the social breakdown of the population according to professions and income, and which areas will develop industry and which housing. He stored all the important facts about the areas he visited in his mind.

During the following few months he covered the territory of San Jose and Gilroy, the southern and northern part of the Peninsula, the San Rafael-Sonoma area, the sea coast around Santa Cruz, and Contra Costa county up to Lafayette and Walnut Creek. He was amused when they showed him properties with love nests and game houses, well protected in hidden places--all for sale. Soon he was asking the right questions: how much is the annual precipitation, which winds bring fog and rain, how many days are sunny, what is the water source, is this an incorporated district or out in the county, what are the taxes on land or house, how strict are the zoning regulations, and where are the existing highways or where will the planned ones be built? While the real estate agents wanted to impress him, he really was impressed: by the values and prices of houses, properties, open fields, flat pastures, land covered with redwoods, orchards, or old decaying vineyards. They were all very, very expensive.

Fr. Egon was looking for an old, large mansion with many open acres for sale. He learned on the East coast that such places became too expensive to keep up because they needed many household servants and gardeners; therefore religious orders, especially sisters, were buying them up. The sisters worked without household help and were able to do it inexpensively. Fr. Egon couldn't find such buildings or properties here in California. In the long run, it was for the best, whatever they had to build would be according to their needs and would be functional for the school. Old buildings constantly needed changes and repairs when turned into schools.

The more he learned of real estate and the property values in California, the more disheartened he became. The land on the market started at two thousand dollars per acre in acceptable places, going to six and eight thousand when there was a view or a few trees. Prices of property zoned for business went far out of consideration. He was frightened, how could he ever persuade his colleagues to move to California when in the East or in the Midwest the value of property was ten times less. His only consolation at that time was that they did not have the money anyway; they could buy nothing. Therefore he had a duty to look for benefactors. Some substantial donation would convince his fellow priests to make the move to California.

As the months passed, Fr. Egon loved the Golden State more and more. His first winter brought plenty of rain, even some floods, but the beauty of nature, the blue skies, the balmy air, the bright sunshine, the Sequoias, the flowers and gardens and the type of life he found here made him feel more and more at home. He pushed away any thought connected to a return to the East.

The monk soon decided that the place of their foundation must be in California. The chancery office showed interest in the Benedictines because they were educators. He became convinced that here in California, they could succeed with a high school. He also saw that to persuade his confreres to settle in such an expensive area, he must get some initial financial support.

CHAPTER VI

INTERLUDE IN MARIN COUNTY

ONE EVENING, while living with the Franciscan fathers in San Francisco, Fr. Egon sat next to Fr. Brendan Mitchell at the dining room table, who was the editor of the Franciscan periodical, "Way," and director of the Third Order of St. Francis in the West. When Fr. Mitchell learned from the dinner conversation why Fr. Egon was there, he suddenly remembered that a good friend of his, a young and quite influential lady with many children, was looking desperately for a religious order of men who would be willing to operate an elementary school for boys in the city. Fr. Mitchell escorted her to the chancery office to support her request, but at the time no religious order in the archdiocese was interested in such a project. There were several good elementary schools in the city, but all were in the hands of sisters. Fr. Egon knew well that his group had no experience in grade school teaching, and most likely they never would do it. However, the idea that somebody sought the education of boys grabbed his attention. The sons of the same lady will be older soon and she will be interested in good education at the secondary level. Without hesitation he asked Fr. Mitchell to inform his friend about the Benedictines and introduce him to her if possible. The Franciscan father kindly offered his help. He could do it without any imposition since they were childhood neighbors and friends. Fr. Egon moved to Cupertino before Fr. Mitchell could fulfill his promise.

With the approach of Christmas, Fr. Egon visited the Franciscan fathers, expressing again his gratitude for their fine hospitality. He wrote a few lines to Fr. Mitchell, too, reminding him of their previous conversations and repeating his request. In his prompt answer, Fr. Mitchell assured him that he had not forgotten his promise, but the lady had been out of town for a long period and the busy Christmas season had come. After the holidays he mailed the name and address of his friend, who was expecting a phone call from Fr. Egon. With this information, Fr. Egon called her and asked for an appointment, which she promptly arranged.

She was Mrs. Richard K. Miller, born Ann Russell, the only daughter of Mr. Donald Russell, the president of the Southern Pacific Railroad. Her husband was also a member of a prominent Catholic family in the city, a young executive of the Pacific Gas and Electric Company. They had five children at the time (later eight) when Fr. Egon rang the doorbell of their elegant home on Locust Street in San Francisco.

Mrs. Miller was very friendly. With the social ease of a person used to meeting priests from her childhood, she explained to Fr. Egon how she was looking for a religious order of men to teach discipline to her sons and to the sons of her friends. She wrote to different orders but all refused her request, even the local chancery office. In her frustration she turned to the Madames of the Sacred Heart and persuaded them to open a grammar school for boys and hire male teachers for their instruction. This school was already in operation next to their girls' school on Broadway in

San Francisco. It was not exactly what she and her friends had in mind, but it was a satisfactory solution, especially because they could drive their sons and daughters to the same place. When Fr. Egon brought up the question of higher education after grammar school, she told him that the Jesuits and the Christian Brothers had good high schools for boys in the city. Mrs. Miller assured him that she would contact him later, if and when she found some interest among her friends in the Order of St. Benedict. Fr. Egon thought this promise to be a polite but final farewell. He was wrong. Mrs. Miller was a prominent member of high society in San Francisco and had many friends, especially young couples with sons who wanted a good education. When she told them about this meeting with Fr. Egon she learned, to her surprise, that many young husbands knew of the scholarly reputation of the Benedictines, some of whom were graduates of Benedictine schools in the East. Thus the news went around in the Catholic society of San Francisco, that a group of Benedictines was willing to open a school in the archdiocese.

About one month after his visit, at the beginning of February, Mrs. Miller called Fr. Egon at the parish in Cupertino. She explained vividly that she had some good news. Fr. Egon was so excited he hardly could understand the fast speech of Mrs. Miller. She spoke about a property for sale in Marin County that would do well for school purposes and many Catholic families would want to support a private Catholic school for boys in that area. She made a date with Fr. Egon to show him the place.

The property in question was the Hallinan estate in the town of Ross. The owner, Mr. Vincent Hallinan, was well known to all newspaper readers in the Bay Area. His name, or that of one of his sons, was constantly in the papers. A lapsed Catholic, as a lawyer he was the defender, protector, and promoter of all the pink, leftist, extreme, or communist causes, and he was very outspoken against the Catholic Church.

Father Egon studied maps and drove with understandable excitement over the Golden Gate Bridge to Marin County. Mrs. Miller could not be present at the appointed time, but she sent one of her friends, Mrs. Richard P. Cooley, to guide Fr. Egon to the Hallinan estate. It was located on a narrow winding road in a residential area of Ross. A dignified retired general, now in real estate, took them around. Surrounded by well-kept lawns and a rose garden, the two story, twelve bedroom, seven-bathroom mansion, with a good size gym and swimming pool, rested on less than five acres.

This gym made the place especially attractive for school purposes. Mr. Hallinan had five healthy, tough boys, and for them he built a gym next to the swimming pool. It contained showers and dressing rooms and included an indoor tennis court and boxing ring. For tax deduction purposes the place was open to the public, and the noisy friends of the Hallinan boys arrived in their more noisy cars, much to the distress of the neighbors.

Fr. Egon looked over the whole place carefully and asked many questions concerning the water, heating, upkeep, and taxes. He detected in the reading room the collected works of Stalin, in expensive leather binding, ostentatiously placed on an otherwise empty bookshelf. The price of the property was $120,000, quite high but not too bad considering all the assets of the estate.

Fr. Egon evaluated the Hallinan estate with cool objectivity. The location was not the best. It was only a fifteen-minute drive from the Golden Gate Bridge, but the site was in a well-to-do residential area. The zoning did not exclude a school permit because only a fence separated the estate from the well-known Katharine Branson private high school for girls. Even so, the neighbors on an otherwise quiet and narrow street would not welcome the noise and traffic of a school. The property was too small for expansion, for future development, but it would do well for the beginning. A few classrooms could easily be added to the gym, and the mansion could serve as dormitory for a year or two. After a few years, when the school was established and known, it could transfer to a larger and better location without losing students or friends. The greatest impediment was the proximity of Marin Catholic High School, only two miles away. The newest and most expensively built school of the diocese, it was the apple of the archbishop's eye. Fr. Egon saw the difficulties, but here was an opportunity to open a school. He could not let this chance pass by. He must present it to the archbishop and learn his opinion.

Fr. Egon returned to the chancery office, to Msgr. Maher. The chancellor listened attentively to his presentation and channeled him over to the education department. There Msgr. Brown heard the same story. It was obvious that they did not like the location so close to Marin Catholic High School.

Msgr. Brown, the superintendent of the Catholic schools, in spite of his nervous appearance and quick movements, was always very generous with his time and sincerely friendly to the Benedictine Order. Fr. Egon now had the opportunity to explain to him his findings around the Modesto area. He emphasized the positive values of Benedictine education; and the necessity that such a school as they intended to open must be close to San Francisco. He used all his skill to prove the advantages of a Benedictine education. A small school would appeal to a different type of parent, especially a boarding school. It would attract students from a larger area, and the diocesan high school in Marin would not lose students. A lay group wanted that location, and their desire could hardly be ignored by the archdiocese. Msgr. Brown accepted the merits of these arguments and decided to present this plan to the archdiocesan school board and to his Excellency, the archbishop.

The archbishop called Fr. Egon to his office on February 29, 1956. This was an unusually long interview, lasting longer than one hour. Archbishop Mitty brought up many objections to the proposed location and to the type of the future school. Fr. Egon seemingly gave him reasonable answers, because, instead of dismissing the whole case, he promised to ask the opinion of his consultors.

Fr. Egon visited the consultors without delay to prepare them for the approaching meeting and to present to them the plans for the school. He had a long visit in San Rafael with Msgr. McAllister, the most important pastor in Marin County and the most ardent supporter of Marin Catholic High School. The monsignor appreciated Fr. Egon's explanations, did not see any conflict, and promised his support.

At that time Fr. Egon informed Fr. Brunner of this new development. He described the Hallinan estate, the advantages and the difficulties and the reaction of the chancery office in a long letter. Since Easter was approaching, he asked Fr. Brunner to fly to California during the Easter vacation, introduce himself to the archbishop, and take over the negotiations as the senior of the Hungarian Benedictine fathers in the United States. Fr. Brunner did not share the premature enthusiasm of Fr. Egon and declined to come.

The meeting of the archbishop with his consultors did not take place until April 10. According to Msgr. Brown all the consultors were in favor of a small Benedictine boarding school in Ross. Others in the clergy, non-consultors, and especially the principal of Marin Catholic, were against it.

Fr. Egon waited for the official answer of Archbishop Mitty, which did not come. The archbishop was old, in poor health, and nobody could move him. Many important cases were pending in the chancery office and the case of the Benedictines was important only to Fr. Egon. After waiting for nine days, he went boldly to the chancery office and asked for an appointment on April 19. The archbishop received him and they spent another long hour together in lively conversation. The secretary came in four times to announce the arrival of other scheduled visitors, but his Excellency still kept Fr. Egon in his office. The archbishop admitted that the educational department and the consultors were not against the plan, therefore, he did not bring up objections opposing the location of the school. His main concern was the future success of such a school. He brought up the fact that he had to close such a school in the archdiocese in the past, in the 1930's. Fr. Egon learned later that he was speaking of a diocesan boarding school, started by a secular priest with the help of lay teachers. The priest was not well qualified for this job, and did not have the right helpers or support. The school became a refuge for problem children and ran into all kinds of difficulties. Fr. Egon had the courage to point out to his Excellency that 26 years later the situation was different. The population has increased; there were more families interested in good education now, and therefore greater hope for better support. He could not think of failure, when not one person but a group of Benedictines was taking the responsibility. Even in the event of failure, the Benedictine Order, and not the archdiocese, would carry the blame.

The delicate question of finances came up at this time. Most secular priests do not know the structure of the Benedictine Order, in which each abbey is independent. They imagine all orders centralized, like the Jesuits. Obviously this was in the minds of the archbishop and the monsignors as they did not press the question of finances before. Although they knew a small refugee group of monks could not be in possession of substantial capital, they visualized the great and ancient Benedictine Order behind them, backing their endeavor. This time Fr. Egon had to admit that local support was very important to them from the beginning. Instead of emphasizing their poverty, he brought up the value of the Hallinan estate, asking: which religious group, even among the well-to-do, would not go after such a value when offered? Would the archdiocese let such an opportunity slip away? This interesting interview ended with the promise of his Excellency that he would talk a second time with his consultors and would give his final answer later. Thus Fr. Egon remained in suspense for more long weeks.

His Excellency held the second meeting with his consultors on May 8. They positively supported the plan without exception. However, it was too late. A few days earlier a local group in Ross put a down payment on the Hallinan estate, also with the intention to use it for a school. The Benedictines lost. Fr. Egon felt downhearted and beaten. However, it was for the best. He understood later the help of Divine Providence when he learned that the local group in Ross ran into the vehement opposition of the residents, and the town enacted a zoning regulation against a school in that location.

CHAPTER VII

SOCIAL CONTACTS

FROM THE BEGINNING OF FEBRUARY to the middle of May, Fr. Egon concentrated all his work around the Hallinan estate. Although this was lost, the efforts of the past months were not without positive results.

While the negotiations were going on, he had to visit the chancery office often. He met the auxiliary bishops: Merlin J. Guilfoyle, later bishop of Stockton, California, and Hugh A. Donohue, future bishop of Fresno, who showed genuine interest in the Benedictine Order. He also met the consultors whose support was very important. He had opportunities to talk to the members of the educational department and to priests who taught in the schools of the archdiocese. He succeeded in developing a good rapport with the key persons: Msgr. Maher, the chancellor, and Msgr. Brown, the superintendent of Catholic schools. During the long conversations and cheerful chats they learned to know each other better. The monsignors told frank stories about the habits and customs of the archbishop. They learned more about the Benedictines, especially about the group that intended to move into the archdiocese. Fr. Egon could return to the chancery office with a feeling of confidence that he had friends there who promoted his cause before the priests and before his Excellency.

The Marin interlude helped to clarify the future location of the Benedictine school. It had to be in the vicinity of San Francisco. Nobody ever mentioned the Central Valley or Modesto anymore.

During this time he found the early friends and benefactors of the future Woodside Priory and School. Mrs. Richard K. Miller was responsible for raising the interest of a few families in the Benedictines. Among them were those who wanted to establish the school in Ross. Mrs. Richard P. Cooley, who had taken Fr. Egon to the Hallinan estate, had invited him to their home in Ross. Her husband was one of the vice-presidents of the American Trust Company in San Francisco. They had three children at that time (later two more). Sheila Cooley came from the East, she was the 13th child of 14 in the prestigious McDonnell family in New York. One of her sisters was the first wife of Henry Ford II. All of her religious relatives and friends were either members of the Jesuit Order or the Madames of the Sacred Heart. Fr. Egon had no connections and little knowledge of the Jesuits in the East but he was well acquainted with the Madames of Manhattanville College when this was located in Harlem and when they moved to Purchase, N.Y. He was instrumental in getting a chaplaincy there for his confrere, Fr. Stanley, when the latter lost his voice and could not teach any longer in St. Vincent Archabbey, Latrobe, Pennsylvania. Fr. Stanley was still living at the college, preparing for his second doctorate at Fordham when Mrs. Cooley and Fr. Egon exchanged reminiscences about the Madames of the Sacred Heart at Purchase. One other topic kept the conversation going even more at this first meeting. When Fr. Egon told her that he taught at St. Mary's Abbey in Morristown before coming to California, Mrs. Cooley suddenly asked him whether he knew the Carmelite nuns there. By coincidence he was the confessor of the Carmelite Sisters for three years in Morristown and could tell many charming stories about those holy nuns living in enclosure. It turned out that Mrs. Cooley's mother was one of the principal supporters of that convent and even had a hot line with the first prioress, Mother Magdalene.

Mr. Cooley was not at home but in his office on this afternoon. He called Fr. Egon a few days later and made an appointment with him at the Pacific Union Club in San Francisco. The tall, lean, young banker with one arm was 34 years old when Fr. Egon first met him. Ten years later he was the president of Wells Fargo Bank. Mr. Cooley was also from the East, although his family had roots in California as well. He finished high school in three years at Portsmouth Priory, and as a Benedictine graduate he was the first to become interested when he heard from Mrs. Miller about the plans of the Hungarian Benedictines.

Mr. Cooley was a student and played football at Yale University when World War II called him for active duty. As an air force pilot, under the cloudy skies of Belgium, he had to test a special plane. This was not his duty; he was filling in for somebody else. The plane proved to be faulty, and Mr. Cooley bailed out. He parachuted down over the Benedictine Abbey of Maredsous. In this accident he lost his right arm. The military hospital where he recovered was next to the abbey. He visited almost daily with the Benedictines, and, as a former Benedictine student, he felt at home in the abbey: he attended services, made friends among the fathers, and learned about their life and liturgy. He developed a liking for the monastic way of life. However, on returning to the United States, where he was received as a young war hero in the lively society life, his religious vocation faded. Soon he was engaged and married.

He had a polite but searching approach when he first met Fr. Egon at the Pacific Union Club. He told about his Benedictine education and background and his happy memories of Portsmouth Priory School. In the Belgian Abbey of Maredsous, which Fr. Egon knew also, he had found peace, consolation, and new hope for life after he lost his right arm and his outlook for the future was gloomy.

Mr. John E. Cahill, a family member of the great Cahill Construction Company and Mr. Cooley's friend, arrived, and all retired to a quiet corner for a longer conversation. Fr. Egon had to give them the background of the Hungarian Benedictines, their schools before the communist takeover, the fathers who were in the United States, and their qualifications. He frankly revealed to them their need for financial support. He had to answer many questions directed to him from both of these clever, experienced American businessmen in a cool, professional way. Neither of them revealed any emotions during the long session. Fr. Egon never knew whether they were pleased to hear what he said or were disappointed. They spoke frankly of what they would expect from a Benedictine school here in the West. Mr. Cooley had asked the Benedictines of Portsmouth to send a faculty to California and open a school. Now he could write to them, "Do not come," because his prayers were answered, and he had found a Benedictine family.

In the person of Mr. Cooley, Fr. Egon found a very able and most loyal friend of the Priory in California. In time they became personal friends also. Fr. Egon was his confessor for a decade, baptized his fifth child, and took part in many of the joys and sorrows of the family. He could turn to Mr. Cooley for advice and help with confidence. He found him generous with his time even when he held the demanding position of president of Wells Fargo Bank. The first and most loyal supporters of the Priory in the early years were Mr. Cooley's relatives and friends.

Mr. Cahill, like Mr. Cooley, lived in Marin County. He also had sons. They expressed their interest in having the school of the Benedictines close to their homes. They gave encouragement to

Fr. Egon that they would be able to find other families with sons who would have the same outlook and expectations for the education of their children as they did. The men also said they would muster solid financial support for the Benedictines.

Fr. Egon met Mr. Richard K. Miller at his home. Soon the many influential members of the Miller family were also backing the Benedictine fathers.

The name of Mr. Emmet Cashin, Jr. should be mentioned here, also. Although Fr. Egon met him first in business dealings, he soon became a good friend and able promoter of the Benedictines. He was a member of the large realty firm, Fox and Carskadon, later owner of the firm. He took Fr. Egon around and showed him many good properties in the Palo Alto and Menlo Park areas. He personally knew many of the socially prominent owners of those properties, too. He introduced Fr. Egon to Mr. Michael Tobin in San Francisco; the Tobins owned the Hibernia Bank. Mr. Tobin explained proudly that their bank gave many loans to Catholic institutions in Northern California, and they had never lost a penny on those loans. It was Emmet Cashin who later took Fr. Egon to the Burlingame Country Club.

With the acquaintance of the Cooleys, Cahills, Millers, Tobins, and Cashins, Fr. Egon fell into the circle of socially prominent Catholic families in and around San Francisco; those who had further access to connections and financial support. Some of the sons of these families were later students of the Woodside Priory School, for shorter or longer periods.

CHAPTER VIII

PORTOLA VALLEY

AFTER THE MEETING WITH MR. COOLEY AND MR. CAHILL, Fr. Egon mailed a long letter to his confreres. He informed them in detail of the progress made in the chancery office, how he had found a nucleus of a potential local supporting group, and the possibilities and expectations in Ross with the Hallinan estate. He asked the consent and approval of his colleagues for further negotiations with the ecclesiastical and the lay group in the diocese of San Francisco. He made it clear to them that the location, the vicinity of San Francisco, but also the type of work they would do, high school teaching, had become a reality for their future. Future negotiations would impose serious obligations on the Hungarian Benedictine fathers. This letter had some influence on Fr. Brunner. He decided to fly from New York to San Francisco and announced his visit for the end of May. Shortly after Fr. Brunner received the letter all the hopes built around the Hallinan estate collapsed. Fr. Egon informed him without delay, giving the causes of the failure, but asked him to come anyway.

Fr. Egon was now in a difficult situation. For the last three months he had concentrated all of his efforts on the Marin plan. Because of this he neglected to pursue other possibilities on the Peninsula. Now all his labors and toils seemed to be futile, the time wasted.

Just then, when he felt so downhearted, he received a letter from the pastor of his home parish in Hungary. It was May 21, 1956. He opened it and started to read: "Today, on Sunday after the feast of the Ascension, the Saviour, who returned to heaven, called your mother there too, to make her partake of His heavenly glory." He read it and re-read it several times. His mind registered the words, but his heart refused to accept the message. Finally he understood: his mother, Gizella Bendy Javor, age 66, died on May 13, 1956. The pain of the loss of his good mother wiped out the losses of his hopes and expectations in California.

Fr. Egon mourned his dear mother sincerely. He always attributed his religious vocation to her prayers. Becoming a widow at the age of 31, she brought up her five children with an unselfish spirit of motherly sacrifice. Never too strong in health, she had her share of many sufferings and hardships during her earthly life. Fr. Egon saw her the last time in November 1948, on the eve of his escape from Hungary. Now he would never see her gentle face again.

He found consolation remembering her deep faith, her prayerful life. She died fortified with the last rites, praying the Angelus that Sunday at noon. Her pastor finished the letter to Fr. Egon with these words: "Earth became poorer, heaven richer, with a good mother. Jesus shed tears at the death of Lazarus. You will weep too. But have no doubt about her salvation." Fr. Egon felt secure about the eternal salvation of his mother in heaven. He knew this when suddenly the future of the Priory started gradually to unfold, step by step, without difficulties or obstacles. He saw the guiding hand and felt the helping prayers of his mother.

After the loss of the Marin plan and before the arrival of Fr. Brunner, he returned to the places of his earlier explorations. This brought him back to the valley where the gallant Spanish captain, Gaspar de Portola, led the famous expedition that discovered the Bay of San Francisco in 1770, and which was named after him, Portola Valley.

Long before Mrs. Miller contacted him to visit the Hallinan estate, he drove around with Emmet Cashin in the Palo Alto, Menlo Park and Redwood City area. Mr. Cashin showed him the beautiful lands of St. Patrick Seminary, and of the Sacred Heart School and he could not understand why the archbishop or the Madames of the Sacred Heart would not offer to donate a few acres of the large open territories for a good Catholic Benedictine high school. He took Father Egon to Hidden Valley, and they walked over the attractive flat acres of the large Ormandale Ranch owned by Mr. McDounough. The majestic hillside of the 1300-acre Neylan estate, from the top of the Skyline down to the bottom of the valley was a striking sight. The many acres of Mrs. William Gilmore, on the northern edge of Woodside, although hilly, also were desirable and worthy. All of these were located in the county at the time and incorporated into Woodside and Portola Valley years later. Mr. Emmet Cashin knew not only these fine estates, but also their owners. He mentioned them by name, emphasized their Catholic background and their different generosities. He encouraged Fr. Egon to see these gentlemen and present them with his problem.

After some investigation Fr. Egon learned that Mr. McDounough was selling the Ormandale lands of the beautiful Hidden Valley in large blocks. Mr. Gilmore was involved, through his daughters, in promoting the Sacred Heart School in Menlo Park with his charities.

Mr. John Francis Neylan, the famous lawyer of the Hearst family and regent of the University of California, owned the Corte Madera estate (later incorporated in Portola Valley). Fr. Egon found his office in downtown Palo Alto and asked for an appointment. Mr. Neylan was friendly and very generous with his time at their first meeting. He knew well the history and reputation of the Order of

St. Benedict and had visited some old abbeys—or their ruins—in England and France. He was a graduate of Seton Hall University in South Orange, which Fr. Egon knew well from his years in New Jersey. Mr. Neylan paid attention to the story of Fr. Egon and was not unsympathetic to the idea of establishing the Benedictine Order in California on his property. At least this was the impression of Fr. Egon. Because part of his land was on the market on option, he told Fr. Egon to return to see him in a month or so.

When Fr. Egon drove up to the high elevation of Mr. Neylan's Corte Madera estate, studying the territory and the environment, and looked down to the valley, his eyes rested on the rolling hills on the other side of the road where the Priory would one day be located. Although he learned from different sources that Mr. Neylan was selling his land in large blocks, 200 to 300 acres, and the price was about $5,000 to 6,000 per acre, he was dreaming of a donation. A gift of land would bring his confreres here, would convince the archbishop of the location and would be a solid basis for their future he thought.

When he returned to the office of Mr. Neyland he was informed that the old gentleman was sick and recovering in Arizona and not expected back soon. In the following months the Marin project occupied the mind of Fr. Egon. Only in the middle of May, with the visit of Fr. Brunner arranged and his hopes in Marin dashed, did he return to Mr. Neylan. At the occasion of this second meeting, Mr. Neylan was not in good health and not in the best of moods, either. Fr. Egon explained to him politely but frankly that his group did not have the money to buy hundreds of acres at such a high price. He asked Mr. Neylan whether he would consider the donation of a few flat acres for a Benedictine school, just to promote the beginning. Later his group would be able to approach him with a better business proposition. Mr. Neylan laughed and answered jokingly, telling Fr. Egon that the archbishop has much more land than he has, and the archbishop should be the one obliged to make such a donation to the Benedictine fathers in the interest of a good private school.

From the Marin incident Fr. Egon learned that the location should be a good distance from any other Catholic high school to obtain the consent of the diocese. From Mr. Neylan's words he became convinced that he should stop dreaming about a donation of property. His group, the Benedictines, must buy the land themselves, open the school on their own property, and expect support or any kind of donation only after they were established and earned the gifts by the merits of their work. These thoughts were crystallized and fixed in his mind before the arrival of Fr. Brunner.

Even after the refusal of Mr. Neylan, he returned to Portola Valley. He visited his friends, the Gerard de Potteres, who moved from Palo Alto and built their new home there, close to Our Lady of the Wayside church. Fr. Egon knew the family in Europe and baptized two of their children, one in Europe, the other in the United States. During the conversation, Fr. Egon told the family that since he could not obtain a land donation for the Benedictine school, there was nothing else left than to buy some property for the start. Speaking of property, Mrs. de Potteres called his attention to a sign on Portola Road, opposite Mr. Neylan's Corte Madera, which read, "18 acres for sale by owner." He inspected the place with Emmet Cashin and obtained the necessary information about these 18 acres before the visit of Fr. Brunner.

Chapter IX

Agreement with the Archbishop

It was Thursday noon, May 31, 1956, when Fr. Brunner arrived in San Francisco. He stepped out from the airport into the bright sunshine in a white straw hat–so traditional for the clergy on the East coast–and with a black umbrella in his hand. Fr. Egon smiled and blamed himself; he had forgotten to inform him that the rainy season was over in California. Fr. Brunner looked tired at the end of the academic year, and felt dizzy from the long flight.

Fr. Egon introduced him at the parish in Cupertino, where they had lunch, then drove to Santa Cruz. A reservation had been made there for Fr. Brunner at a vacation place run by sisters, and he had a few days to rest. Fr. Egon had parish duties during the weekend, but he visited Fr. Brunner at the beginning of the next week and found him rested and in good disposition to get organized and follow a plan for the next important days.

They talked over all the work Fr. Egon had done here on the West coast. He informed Fr. Brunner in detail about the situation, the possibilities, and especially about the persons he had to meet.

The prices of real estate in California sounded incredibly high in comparison to prices in the East. Fr. Brunner was convinced that Fr. Egon was rather naive and that big-talking real estate agents had fooled him. To eliminate this suspicion, Fr. Egon arranged a meeting with Fr. Raymond Maher. He was the brother of the chancellor, Msgr. Leo Maher, and the procurator of the two large seminaries and their lands in the diocese. His practical local knowledge and personal experience convinced Fr. Brunner of the real value of land in this part of California.

They spent the next two days under the guidance of real estate agents showing Fr. Brunner some properties for sale. Mr. Joseph Pon from Cupertino had previously called Fr. Egon's attention to a beautiful portion of land for sale in the open territory on the northern edge of Saratoga. From there they continued to see the choice property of the Ormandale-Hidden Valley, the Corte Madera ranches, the Gilmore property in the Woodside area, and finally the 18 acres of Mr. Gillson in Portola Valley. As many parcels were sold in blocks at very high prices, Fr. Brunner naturally chose the smallest and least expensive Gillson property.

The next step was to pay a visit to the chancery office and the educational department of the diocese and to ask for an appointment with the archbishop. Fr. Brunner got a very friendly reception at these places at the time of his introduction.

After a week in Santa Cruz, Fr. Brunner moved to San Francisco. As he had lived in a Franciscan parish in New York, he got an introduction and an invitation from the Franciscan fathers to stay with them in St. Anthony's parish in San Francisco. This location was more convenient to reach the chancery office and to meet people. He could also visit the city while Fr. Egon performed parish duties in Cupertino.

They had an appointment with his Excellency on June 15 and found him in an exceptionally friendly mood. After polite remarks, the conversation turned to business. Archbishop Mitty made it clear that any religious group in his diocese must agree to his terms. First of these was that the Benedictines must accept parish obligations, i.e., to help the parishes in the vicinity with pastoral work, mostly with confessions and Masses on weekends. This was not new, and not difficult, a term easy to agree to. The second was the question of the chapel or future church of the Benedictines. As a very old and exempt order, the Benedictines always had their churches open to the public. Multitudes of people from great distances visited many of the large abbey churches to hear Gregorian chants and participate in fine liturgy, and many were famous pilgrim destinations for centuries. Archbishop Mitty knew well that an open church of the Benedictines would attract people here, and as a consequence parish attendance would suffer. Therefore he demanded that the Benedictines renounce their privilege to keep their church open to the public. This was not an easy decision. Fr. Egon and the archbishop had discussed it previously. The Benedictines had the right and could defend this right by appealing to Rome. But who wishes to fight an archbishop, especially when he is granting a permit to move into his diocese? The Benedictine fathers had to compromise. They knew it would take years, anyway, before they would have a community and a church large enough to attract people to their services. As long as the students of the school and their parents, or the inner circle of friends, may use the chapel, it would suffice to have just a semi-public status. Later, after many years, with another archbishop, their successors may clear up this matter. They renounced their right to a church open to the public.

Now they had to present the location of the school. Fr. Egon was cautious. He knew well that it had to be a decent distance from other Catholic high schools. He also knew that it could not be close to Menlo Park, as this small community already had large tax exempt estates because of St. Patrick's Seminary and the Sacred Heart School. He presented the map of the area and his Excellency saw that Serra, the diocesan high school in San Mateo, and St. Francis, the high school of the Holy Cross Brothers in Mountain View, were about 15 miles away from the selected site. Also, it was not located in any incorporated town, but in open territory of San Mateo County. His Excellency accepted this Portola Valley location without objections.

The archbishop specified the type of school: it should be rather small, with quality education, small classes, and a rather high tuition. The diocese did not yet have a Catholic school of this type so it would be an asset and fill a need. Kept small and expensive, it would not attract students who would go to the existing Catholic high schools. Finally they agreed on the opening of the school for September 1957. The fairness of Archbishop Mitty impressed Fr. Brunner. He did not expect to make a deal when he flew out to California and now one was ready at the first occasion on which he met the archbishop.

Msgr. Brown and Msgr. Maher were amazed and pleased to experience this easy and friendly disposition and rather unexpected quick action of their archbishop. Not to lose any time, Msgr. Brown offered the secretarial services of his office, and they wrote the petition of the Benedictines according to the terms of the archbishop, and prepared and forwarded it to his Excellency for final approval on the same date: June 15, 1956.

The two chancery officials congratulated the Benedictines fathers and assured them of success.

The rest was the regular deskwork of the ecclesiastical bureaucracy. They would answer the petition on official and sealed documents with the signature of the archbishop.

The petition presented to the archbishop revealed the sarcasm or the sense of humor of Fr. Brunner. When his Excellency did not want to give the right of a public chapel or church to the Benedictines, he explained with many examples the possible friction with local parishes and used the expression "detrimental" concerning the religious house or monastery in his sentence. Fr. Brunner intentionally used the same expression when he wrote in the petition, "It is obvious that we will have a chapel, both for monastic purposes and also as a school chapel. However, we understand completely that a chapel open to the public might be seriously detrimental to the welfare of the parish and to the spiritual welfare of the people in the area. Hence we resign the privilege of opening our chapel to the public..." Neither Msgr. Brown nor Fr. Egon noticed the full weight of this expression at the time, although they read the text repeatedly before it was typed in the final form. The passing years proved well that the Priory did not become "detrimental" to the spiritual welfare of the people in the area.

When Mr. Cooley learned that Fr. Brunner was in San Francisco, he wanted to meet him. He, Mr. John Cahill and the two Benedictines had lunch together at the Sheraton Palace Hotel. The agreement with the archdiocese pleased these gentlemen, and they were interested in the location. Mr. Cahill's parents owned a summer place in Woodside, and he knew the area. He agreed to join Fr. Egon to inspect the property on Portola Road. They went the next afternoon. They walked around and climbed the hill; Mr. Cahill, most impressed with the location, also liked the price. "It's a steal for that price." With this opinion, Fr. Brunner was assured and finally convinced that Fr. Egon was not fooled by the real estate prices. The two monks did not mention finances at this meeting. Fr. Egon left the flow of the conversation up to Fr. Brunner who kept this delicate issue discretely out.

As finances were quite important, Fr. Egon cherished hopes that this omission would be corrected at the meeting with Mrs. Miller who received them the next morning. The usually friendly and talkative Mrs. Miller was almost a stranger, completely the opposite of the person whom Fr. Egon prepared Fr. Brunner to meet. She looked very tired, as someone who had not slept for days, and who had no special interest in her visitors or the topic of their conversation. It was impossible to bring up the question of finances or of support for the new school. Finally she realized from the conversation that the school would be located in the vicinity of Woodside. Woodside! She lit up and told the fathers that they must see Mrs. Ralph K. Davies, who lives in Woodside and would be a great help in everything. She called Mrs. Davies without delay and made an appointment for the same morning. Fr. Egon drove Fr. Brunner to Woodside and had a hard time finding the street of the Davies' home. Street signs in those days were very few and not very visible in Woodside.

Mrs. Davies had returned the previous evening from her annual boat trip to the Orient. All the suitcases were still in the lobby of her beautiful mansion, and she was on the terrace with a few friends, opening packages and admiring all the beautiful articles she brought home from the Far East. It was not the best time for her to receive two unknown priests. However, she was gracious and friendly, offered refreshments, and listened to the story of the Hungarian Benedictines who were about to open a school in the vicinity of her home. She must have had hundreds of other things on her mind, her phone ringing, guests coming, the house help and gardeners reporting, but the visit was good for an introduction and she remembered the Benedictines. Fr. Brunner enjoyed her natural kindness and the beauty of her home.

When Fr. Brunner arrived in San Francisco he just wanted to look around in California. He assured Fr. Egon that there was no hurry to start a common religious house for the Hungarian Benedictines, that there were many other places and possibilities in the United States beside San Francisco's archdiocese, and he made it clear that he did not come to make a final agreement with the archdiocese. Fr. Egon wondered why he worked so hard for a whole year if that was Fr. Brunner's idea. Eventually everything went so well that when he returned to the East, he informed the members of the community of the final agreement. All have to prepare to arrive in Portola Valley, California, the summer of 1957, for common monastic life in our own monastery, and for educational work in our own secondary school in the archdiocese of San Francisco.

Fr. Christopher arrived for a short visit in August, 1956.

CHAPTER X

FINALLY: ESTABLISHED

A FEW WEEKS AFTER THE DEPARTURE OF FR. EMOD BRUNNER, Fr. Egon received a letter from his Excellency, the archbishop. The text was as follows:

Dear Father Javor:

I am enclosing the canonical document for the erection of a religious house in the neighborhood of Portola (Valley), California. I would be very grateful if you would send it to Fr. Brunner. Owing to the shortage of priests at the present time I would ask you please to continue your work at Cupertino until other arrangements can be made.

With every best wish and blessing I remain,

Faithfully yours,

John J. Mitty.

At the same time Monsignor Brown also informed Fr. Egon that the final document was ready and signed. Fr. Egon happily forwarded the Latin document, dated July 20, to Fr. Brunner. According to the request of the archbishop he continued to fulfill his parish duties at St. Joseph's. His attention turned to the further steps necessary before the purchase of the property: 1) the Benedictine community had to be incorporated in the state of California, 2) a percolation test had to be made on the property and 3) the use permit of the zoning commission had to be obtained.

The incorporation required three residents of California. As Fr. Egon was the only Benedictine present, he needed to ask the help of the laity. Messr. Richard P. Cooley and Emmet Cashin agreed to place their names on the legal papers to have three residents. For the name of the corporation Fr. Egon just asked "Benedictine Fathers," but to his surprise the answer from Sacramento stated that a corporation already existed under that name in California. (They were from St. Gregory's Abbey of Shawnee, Oklahoma, and did parish work in the archdiocese of Los Angeles.) In a hurry and without much imagination, he asked for and got the title: Benedictine Fathers of the Priory, Inc.

With the possession of a legal title, he could pay the down payment for the property in Portola Valley. The purchase depended on the percolation test and on the permit from the zoning commission. The percolation test was a serious problem. There was no sewer system in the valley in those days and each home had to provide its own septic solution. Planning for a monastery and for a school, one had to be certain about ample septic facilities before the purchase of the land. After long delays the work was done, and, although the hillside proved to be negative, the flat lands were large enough and absorbing enough for septic purposes.

The next step was to apply to the county for a use permit. No institution had existed before in Portola Valley; if the zoning commission should deny the permit, Fr. Egon had to look for another location.

The request of the Benedictine Fathers of the Priory would be on the agenda of the planning commission for their August meeting. Anyone could attend and support a plan, or protest against it.

Mr. Gillson, the owner of the property, explained to Fr. Egon that he had only one "bad" neighbor, Mr. Louis Gambetta, Sr. There had been several border controversies in the past, and Mr. Gillson feared that this neighbor would protest the upcoming sale. Although this was an unfounded suspicion of Mr. Gillson, Fr. Egon had to take precautions and prepare well for the meetings.

Mr. Emmet Cashin, with all the smooth operational skills of a real estate agent, was spreading the news about the Priory and school in the vicinity of the selected location and invited supporting friends to the meeting.

Fr. Egon paid visits to the parishes close to their new home. Fr. Guy Hayden, the pastor of Our Lady of the Wayside church in Portola Valley, received him with open friendliness. He served as pastor in the parish without an assistant. According to his calculation the Catholic population was growing rapidly in his parish, and he bought property in Woodside for a new church, school, and convent. To make the parishioners aware of this plan he started Sunday Masses in Woodside (in the auditorium of the public school), and he needed pastoral help. He welcomed the idea of having a religious house in his parish and wanted to use the assistance of Fr. Egon as soon as he moved into the valley. He always remained most friendly to the Benedictine community, which supplied his needs not only on weekends but also on many occasions of his frequent and sometimes long illnesses. Fr. Egon learned from the parishioners at a later date that a group of them wanted very much to buy the Gillson 18 acres for the parish before the Benedictines made their down payment. They thought it would be desirable for the parish school since it was only a mile away from the church. Fr. Hayden was personally against the choice. (The parish never opened a school, but in later years used the classrooms of the Priory for religious instructions.)

Msgr. Edwin Kennedy was the very important and powerful pastor of St. Raymond's church in Menlo Park. He had chancery background in establishing the diocese in Hawaii and the chiseled manners of priests of bishopric courts. His attitude was quite short and cold with Fr. Egon on the occasion of their first encounter in St. Raymond's rectory. He explained his own importance and his role in letting Benedictines settle in the archdiocese and in Portola Valley, because the archbishop consulted him on this matter. The monsignor made it clear that the Priory got the archbishop's permission with his approval, and the monks must keep this fact in mind. He expected occasional pastoral help and warned Fr. Egon that he should leave his parishioners alone. Although many of his good parishioners became ardent supporters of the Priory, the Benedictines kept peace and friendship with Msgr. Kennedy, and gave him plenty of pastoral help.

The third parish in the area was St. Pius in Redwood City. The pastor of this church was Fr. Fitzsimmons, a native of Ireland, a good friend of Fr. Philip Ryan and a frequent guest in the parish at Cupertino. There he met Fr. Egon often and knew the plans of the Benedictines. During all the years up to his retirement he was a true friend of the Priory and a generous pastor. St. Pius church became a steady mission of the Benedictine monks for about two decades.

The new Priory needed to open a bank account. Because Mr. Richard Cooley was with American Trust Company, which later merged with Wells Fargo Bank, Fr. Egon went to the office of this bank in Menlo Park. The Priory remained with Wells Fargo Bank, using the closer office when it opened on Whiskey Hill Road in Woodside for many years.

There was no mail service in Portola Valley in 1956 and the Priory needed a definite address. Fr. Egon, finding no vacancy for a post office box in Menlo Park, Palo Alto, or Stanford, had to rent one in the more distant Redwood City. The Priory used this until mail delivery service arrived in the valley. From the post office box address, some friends of the Hungarian fathers in Europe, not knowing the exact geographical location, thought that the new Priory was far out in the wilderness. Even Fr. Gerard Bekes thought for a short time that his confreres would be involved in missionary activity in some underdeveloped part of the Wild West. Others, readers of western novels, identified Redwood City with Carson City, Virginia City, or Dodge City, and asked many questions about cowboys, sheriffs, gold, jail, and the lawless conditions of this part of the Wild West.

After the agreement with the archdiocese, the Priory became officially established and needed publicity for the future monastery and school. Through the courtesy of some friends, Fr. Egon got more and more introductions.

In July, Mr. Cooley took him to his important relatives, the Marshall P. Madisons. Their main home was in San Francisco, but they spent some weeks every summer in their homes in Atherton and Carmel. It was in their Atherton home that Fr. Egon met them the first time. Mr. Madison rested on a sofa on the patio. A few days earlier he had fallen off his horse, and he was not able to walk for weeks.

Mrs. Madison said jokingly that this summer was her happiest because her husband had to stay at home. In pleasant surroundings, refreshed with cool drinks, Mr. Cooley introduced the situation of the Hungarian Benedictine fathers to his relatives, explaining discretely that they needed some financial aid for the realization of their plans. Mr. Madison addressed questions to Fr. Egon and finally asked him how much money he needed. Very timidly Fr. Egon answered that they could have a good start with $100,000. "That's easy," said Mr. Madison, "you only have to find ten persons who would give you $10,000 each." Fr. Egon was puzzled at this; on many other such occasions, he could not understand whether such an answer was a joke or was serious. Where could he find ten persons who would donate ten thousand dollars for a Benedictine school? He could not, but Mr. Madison had friends and connections and promised his support. He and his wife became solid friends of the Priory, inviting the fathers to their homes every year regularly and visiting the Priory often. They were generous supporters with their own gifts and by channeling the donations of their friends to the Priory. Mr. Madison, a well-known lawyer, served on the boards of several charitable foundations and used his influence for the benefit of the Priory quite often. Mr. and Mrs. Edward Eyre, relations of the Madisons, became most important in the life of the Priory. It was Mr. Madison who persuaded Mrs. Eyre to start the Gardening Committee to beautify the Priory grounds.

Mrs. Ralph K. Davies' dinner party, also in July, enlarged the circle of the future friends and supporters of the Priory. She mailed an invitation to "all the fathers" and Fr. Egon had to disappoint her, telling her he lived all alone during the work of preparation, and the others would arrive a year later, when the school opened. Several couples from the area were present in her elegant home for this dinner: the Paul Fays, Sr., John R. Kielys, Sam Eastmans, and Philip Fitzgeralds; all became supporters of the Priory. The son of the Fays, Paul Fay, Jr., (Undersecretary of the Navy in the Kennedy administration) was in the paving business and organized a group of contractors in 1957 to build the entrance road, an oiled road from Portola Road to the administration building, and to level the first soccer field. The second son of the Kiely family, Michael, graduated from the second class of the school and the Kiely family was always generous with their help, advice, connections, and with their large annual donations. Mr. Fitzgerald helped in financial planning above his gifts, and his wife was for years one of the pillars of the Gardening Committee. The Eastmans directed their nephew, Gary Eastman, to the opening of the school.

Other important introductions came through the efforts of Mr. Emmet Cashin. As has been mentioned, he took Fr. Egon to the Hibernia Bank in San Francisco. The Priory drew the first and some later loans from the bank, and Michael's son, Joe Tobin, became a Priory graduate. Mr. Emmet Cashin also organized a fine luncheon party at the Burlingame Country Club for a group of prominent ladies of that area. At this occasion Fr. Egon was introduced to Mesdames William Budge, Michael Tobin, Frank McGuinness, her sister, Mrs. John Saidy, Harry Kuchins, the future Mrs. Robert Miller, her sister and others. These families became benefactors in the early years, some of their sons were in the Priory School for summer or regular sessions. The ladies organized several fashion shows, sold tickets for raffles and worked hard for the benefit of the new school. They brought their elderly parents into the circle of benefactors.

In August, Richard Cooley gave a dinner party to promote the Priory. Jokingly he called it a "thousand dollar a plate dinner." The John Cahills, Richard Millers, and Atherton Phlegers were present. The Cahills sent one of their sons to be in the Priory's second class. All directed their own contributions and those of their friends to the Benedictines. The Madisons, Phlegers, and Millers had access to foundations. The Cahills brought Sir Daniel and Countess Bernadine Donohue to the Priory, and their foundation (The Dan Murphy Foundation) channeled very substantial grants for many years to the school.

The session of the county Planning Commission with the Gillson property on the agenda was on August 15, 1956, at 2:00 p.m. Fr. Egon arrived with Mr. Emmet Cashin. Mr. Gillson was present, nervously pointing out his neighbor, Louis Gambetta, Jr., with his lawyer in the audience. Mr. Paul Fay, Sr. and Mrs. John Kiely from Woodside were there for the support of the Priory, also Mr. John Cahill. It was a long session; after sixteen other matters of business there was a break, during which Fr. Egon met the members of the Planning Committee. The chairman was a very good Catholic, Mr. Calan, from Colma, who assured Fr. Egon of success. Mr. Cashin presented the case, emphasizing the importance of a good school run with highly educated professional men, and asked for a use permit for 200 students, at high school level with boarding facilities. Nobody spoke up against it and in five minutes the matter was concluded. The Health Department wanted a report about the septic facilities, after which the County Board of Supervisors gave their final consent. Fr. Egon's evening Mass in the parish of Cupertino on this Feast of the Assumption turned out to be a great Eucharistic thanksgiving. The local papers (Palo Alto, Menlo Park, and Redwood City) printed some reports after the session of the Planning Commission, using only that source for information, proclaiming loudly that "Catholics" will move into the valley with a high school for boys.

After the Feast of Assumption, Fr. Christopher arrived for a visit to appraise the progress and to see the selected site of the future Priory. He spent some days in the parish at Cupertino, and Fr. Egon drove him around showing him the environment of their future activities. The beauty of the region, cleanness of the towns and the bright, clear air of Portola Valley thrilled him. He walked over every inch of the 18 acres, climbed the hill and could not have enough of the fine view. He really loved everything that he saw and could sincerely write an enthusiastic report to the other colleagues.

On Sunday, August 20, the Hungarians celebrated the Feast of St. Stephen in the city, and Fr. Jaszovszky asked Fr. Christopher to be a guest priest and preach the sermon. On that occasion the local Hungarians were introduced to the many excellent homilies, which Fr. Christopher preached to them during the following long years.

That evening, driving up to Skyline Road from the valley, Fr. Christopher and Fr. Egon met Mrs. Otto Oswald. She immediately took them to dinner at their restaurant, the Skywood Chateau, explaining all her connections with the Benedictines in Mount Angel, Oregon. As her sister was a Benedictine nun,

Sr. Flavia, she was delighted with the idea of a Benedictine monastery and school in Portola Valley. Their relations, the Oswalds, Schutzs, and Stadlers, all became good friends and generous benefactors of the Priory. The sons of Ralph Oswald and one grandson of Mrs. Stadler graduated from the Priory School years later. Jack Schutz provided the Community with the daily table wine for years. Joe Stadler and his wife donated property and occasionally their gardening care to clean up the Priory grounds. Having an ecclesiastical goods store in San Francisco, the first chapel equipment, missal, etc., were also their donations.

Fr. Christopher and Fr. Egon had an opportunity to discuss the immediate and future needs of their new priory. They thought it would be useful to prepare a small brochure about the life in the Order of St. Benedict and also some information on the school to be opened by the Benedictines in California. The insignificant, small brochures served their purpose before and during the opening year. The Hungarians in the United States learned about the Benedictine foundation through coverage in the "Catholic Hungarian Sunday," a weekly newspaper. Well pleased with his trip, Fr. Christopher returned to Michigan for one more school year, and he informed the confreres in a long circular letter of his impressions.

In September, Fr. Egon visited the chancery office and asked to be relieved from his parish duties at St. Joseph's. His pastor was eager to get a permanent assistant. The parish was growing rapidly in population and the work was too much for one priest. Msgr. Maher, the chancellor, promised a solution in due time. The official announcements of priestly assignments in the diocese were published at the end of September. A young priest, Fr. Ribera, became the assistant to the pastor at St. Joseph's in Cupertino.

Fr. Brunner authorized him to buy the 18 acres on Portola Road in Portola Valley for $83,000. The fathers did not have the $16,000 for the down payment. A loan for $5,000 from personal friends of Fr. Leopold made this possible. Mr. Cashin's real estate office took care of the paperwork with the title office. The Gillsons were satisfied with the deal at the time; they got the full price for which they offered their property. Only years later, when the land values started to soar in the valley, they became bitter and complained against the Priory for the low price of the sale.

Fr. Egon could not yet occupy the ranch house on their own newly acquired property as the Gillsons, according to the sales agreement, did not have to move until November. He returned often to Portola Valley to walk over their "own" acres.

While he was waiting to occupy the property, the Medical Mission Sisters offered Fr. Egon hospitality in their guesthouse. He spent one month there as their guest, offering daily Mass in the absence of their chaplain, Fr. Switalski.

CHAPTER XI

FURTHER CONTACTS

FREE FROM PARISH DUTIES AND HAVING MORE TIME, Fr. Egon continued his efforts to make the presence of the Benedictines known in the diocese and to gain friends for the support of their school. Of his many trips during this period, two became important for the future: one to Monterey and Carmel, the other to Los Angeles and vicinity.

The most renowned Catholic high school for girls at the time was Santa Catalina in Monterey, under the direction of the Dominican sisters. The well-known private school for boys at the secondary level, Robert Louis Stevenson, owned and run by lay people, was located nearby in Pebble Beach.

Santa Catalina, with its old and new attractive buildings in California-Spanish style, its large chapel and flower gardens, well-kept fields, swimming pool, and tennis courts, looked like a true jewel, an ideal environment for fine education. The gifted principal, Sister Kiernen, took Fr. Egon around and showed him the impressive facilities of the school. She gave precious insight into how the school developed, what high expectations the parents set in return for their financial support, and how they try to keep their student body small and Catholic. It served as consolation to Fr. Egon to hear of the hardships of their beginnings, although the Dominican nuns were established in California long ago and had generations of loyal, supporting alumni. This school for girls became a natural recruiting place for Priory students; sons of the same Catholic families, whose daughters attended Santa Catalina, later went to the Priory. The two schools kept in contact with each other during the first decade of the Priory. They had many social events, dinners, and dances together.

Robert Louis Stevenson School for boys also offered a splendid view with the green fields and tall pine trees on its large campus at Pebble Beach. Beside the location, it enjoyed one other advantage: the choice of teachers. Many retired educators lived in the vicinity of Carmel and were willing to continue to work as part-time teachers in the school. In spite of the famous name and high tuition, the school did not have much to offer in buildings and equipment in those days. This observation also served as consolation to Fr. Egon. In the early years of the Priory, Robert Louis Stevenson School became the only rival in soccer, and their semi-annual matches were great events in the lives of both schools.

Monterey was also the location of the renowned language school of the U.S. Army. Fr. Egon used the opportunity to visit the Hungarian department of this language school to become acquainted with its teachers, methods, and fine modern equipment. Later, groups of soldiers from the Hungarian department came to visit the Priory and practice the language with the Hungarian fathers.

The elegant La Playa hotel in Carmel belonged to Mr. Stanley. He and his Hungarian wife (former actress Iren Biller) offered a friendly reception and dinner to Fr. Egon. Mr. Stanley supplied him with introductory letters to his friends in Los Angeles and with much useful advice on how to get around in the southern metropolis of California.

The art colony of Carmel also had a well-known Hungarian, Mr. Geza St. Galy. Fr. Egon visited him in his studio and spent hours with this interesting, well-educated, and successful man. The son of a rich landowner in Hungary, he held university degrees in law and agronomy, but in the United States he survived by the skill he learned as a child from the village potter. His works in ceramics decorated many churches and public buildings, and he had many friends and clients on the San Francisco Peninsula. He promoted the cause of the Benedictines with introductions and by donating some of his works to the Priory. The Byzantine picture of King St. Stephen, the Madonna, Star of the Sea, and other ceramics in the Priory, were his creations and gifts. The Stations of the Cross, also his work, were a gift of Mrs. Herbert Allen (mother of Mrs. Gill).

Returning from Carmel, Fr. Egon discovered a motel in Santa Cruz with a perfectly spelled Hungarian name: Motel Lengyel. He drove in and made his acquaintance with the owners. The Lengyels later donated many useful items: towels, bed linen, carpets, curtains, bedspreads, soap and cleaning materials to the Priory.

Fr. Egon always remembered his first drive to Los Angeles as most pleasant. Finally he was at ease. When he drove from the East toward the West, he was under tension. His mind was heavy with the uncertainty of the future, with the questionable results of his mission, "Is it worthwhile to spend so much time, to go so far, to try to find a solid place for the future foundation?" Now these questions were answered. The diocese accepted them; they owned property in California; they would be together within a year and would open their school the next September. He felt some security as he drove toward the south and could enjoy the scenery: the rolling hills, the green of live oaks over the dried golden grass, and the cloudless blue skies of California. Highway 101 crossed the wide dry bed of the Salinas

River several times while the water flowed underground. Soon he passed King City and the land known as Steinbeck country in American literature. After turning to the south Central Valley toward Fresno, he saw with fascination, for the first time in his life, cotton fields, grapevines grown into large old trees, legions of huge tarantulas criss-crossing the roads, and the lazy rhythmic movements of the oil pumps around Bakersfield. The refreshing view of the citrus groves was all a new sight to him, as were the long avenues with tall majestic palm trees.

While in Los Angeles, he followed the instructions Mr. Stanley gave him in Carmel: 1) to use a car because of the immense distances of the city, 2) to stay in a hotel instead of rectories or private homes in order to receive messages without delay and have the use of a phone always ready for any call, and 3) to select a central location to save time and gas and be able to be prompt for appointments. This advice he followed on later trips he took to promote the cause of the Priory.

These days in Los Angeles proved to be very educational. To his great surprise he heard that another Benedictine was going around in Los Angeles promoting his "new" monastery. He was Father Vincent Martins, looking for a place for the Belgian Benedictines, about to arrive here, forced out of China by the communists. They settled later in Valyermo on the edge of the Mojave Desert.

Fr. Egon soon learned his own shortcomings in the promotion of their monastery and school. He could not answer or had only negative responses to the question: "What is the name of your school?" "Are you incorporated, tax deductible?" He had difficulty giving the location and lacking postal delivery, could not give a definite address, just a post office box number in Redwood City. To those who graduated from Stanford he could mention, "It is farther on up the road from Rosotti's." They all knew the location of that famous beer-drinking place of Stanford students on Alpine Road. He discovered that secretaries kept visitors out and did not let them into the offices of their employers, even with letters of introduction. He learned that Northern California is a "different world" for the "Angelinos." His experience with Dr. Strub, president of Santa Anita Race Track, illustrated this. The doctor had his pen in his hand to write a check for the Priory, when he stopped, looked up and asked, "and where is your place located?" When Fr. Egon explained, "It is in Northern California, not far from San Francisco," he put his pen away, with the explanation that they cannot give support to anything in Northern California, according to their bylaws. Many good people naturally supported the local needs with their charities. On the other hand, the introductory letters of the Stanleys opened doors to people who later supported the Priory generously.

Beside Dr. Strub, Hernando Curtright, the owner of the Beverly Hills Hotel, received him kindly, being acquainted with the Benedictine Order and supporting them in Mexico through his Mexican wife. Rod la Roque, a retired Hollywood film photographer, whose wife, Vilma Banky, was a Hungarian actress, took him around in the circle of his friends and organized an elegant luncheon at the Beverly Hills Country Club. Among the guests present were Dr. and Mrs. Russel Newling, whose daughter was married to Alfred Bloomingdale, founder and head of the Diner's Club credit cards. Although

Mr. Bloomingdale sent his sons to school at Portsmouth Priory, he became a supporter of the Woodside Priory also.

Fr. Egon had a happy reunion with Msgr. Stephen Kerner, who was in good health and served as assistant pastor in a parish at Redondo Beach. He paid his respects at the Hungarian St. Stephen's parish in Los Angeles. By a lucky coincidence the Hungarians had a huge banquet the following Sunday. At that Fr. Egon had an opportunity to make a speech and announce the settling of the Hungarian Benedictines in Northern California. He made some good contacts with members of the Hungarian colony, too. However their donations were soon sent to help the refugees who fled Hungary.

On October 23, he turned into a gasoline station on Sunset Boulevard in Hollywood. To his great surprise he found no one working at this large and clean place; all the attendants huddled before the radio, listening with great concentration. It must be baseball, the World Series, thought Fr. Egon. He left the car and joined the group of listeners. In this way he learned of the revolt that had broken out against the Russians and against the communist regime in Budapest, Hungary. He left Los Angeles and drove back to the Peninsula with heavy heart and great anxiety, knowing that blood was spilling on the streets of Budapest.

Chapter XII

The Interlude of the Hungarian Revolt in 1956

WHEN FR. EGON ARRIVED AT HIS TEMPORARY HOME at the Medical Mission Sisters in Los Altos, the chaplain, Fr. Switalski, presented him in writing all the news he had collected which had seeped out about the revolt in Hungary. This Holy Cross father taught diplomacy at Notre Dame University, and also spent years as a missionary in Pakistan. He was a well read and updated scholar in politics and as interested in the revolt as a Hungarian. During the following two weeks they spent all their free time in front of the television or listening to the radio.

The heroic uprising of a small group of oppressed people against the giant tyrant evoked the admiration of all freedom-loving people. Listening to the news, waves of emotion were storming over the hearts of the Hungarian Benedictines in exile. First, they felt amazement—the unbelievable, the impossible did happen. As they had so many times in the past, the Hungarians stood up again for the cause of freedom. Then they felt joy mixed with national pride. Among all the oppressed satellites, their compatriots had the determination and courage to do it. Then admiration followed. Although intellectuals and writers paved the way, the factory workers and the youth manned the streets and barricades. After eleven years of oppression and indoctrination, those well treated pet-classes of the communist society wanted change and turned against their unwanted rulers, against the tanks of the "liberators." Hope rode high when the Hungarian army sided with the people in the fight against the Russians, when Cardinal Mindszenty was freed, when a new government declared the independent, free national state of Hungary and broke away from the Warsaw Pact countries. After the Iron Curtain rolled up and free communication was established with Western Europe, some of Fr. Egon's confreres in the United States dreamed about returning home and dedicating their energy to rebuilding their country. Then the uplifting news turned into fright, pain, and tears.

At this time, England and France started the war at the Suez Canal. The attention of the world turned from Hungary to Egypt. The Western powers declined to give armed support to the uprising, and the president of the United States assured the Russians of non-intervention. Soon 200,000 fresh Russian troops with modern armor moved into Hungary. On November 4, Budapest was encircled, and in a few days the revolt was defeated. Instead of enjoying desired freedom, the tragic country sank deeper into retaliation and oppression.

The voice of freedom radio, crying for help, was not yet silenced in Budapest when Fr. Egon was unexpectedly in demand on the Peninsula. As a salutary side effect, the sad events in Hungary brought publicity to the Hungarian Benedictines in California. Fr. Egon went before large and small groups for questions and answers in connection with his experiences in communist Hungary. Most of these invitations came from Catholic or parish organizations and some of them deserve special mention.

One day Monsignor Francis Quinn (later bishop of Sacramento), the assistant superintendent of Catholic schools and editor of the diocesan paper, the Monitor, phoned. He urged Fr. Egon to come to the chancery office. There he introduced him to Val King, who worked for the Monitor and moderated the Catholic radio hour. The three of them drove out together and watched the arrival of an aircraft carrier coming majestically through the Golden Gate into San Francisco Bay. The topic of conversation was not the navy, but Fr. Egon's background, his experiences, the situation in Hungary, and the tragic revolt. Driving back to the chancery, Val King declared to Msgr. Quinn, "We have plenty of material." Then the Monsignor invited Fr. Egon to be the guest Sunday afternoon, November 4, on the television program of the archdiocese. In spite of his poor English and horrible pronunciation, he felt it his duty to say yes. His heart was heavy with the sad news from Budapest. Stiff and tense, as anybody would be on a first television interview, he started with understandable nervousness. Slowly he gained his composure, and the half hour passed quickly. Mr. Val King gave a friendly and lengthy introduction, announcing the acceptance of the Hungarian Benedictine fathers by Archbishop Mitty and the opening of their monastery and school the next September in Portola Valley.

Two weeks later, also on a Sunday afternoon, he was on the Stanford University program on Channel 4, in San Francisco. Among the three participants were Dr. Skorakowski from the Hoover Institute, representing Poland; a younger Stanford professor, Czechoslovakia; and Fr. Egon, his native Hungary. He felt more relaxed, although his role was more difficult because, without previous preparation, he had to give instant answers to the questions of the two Stanford moderators. Again the Benedictines were introduced to the audience at the beginning of the program with their plans for a monastery and school, so close to Stanford University.

The foreign students' club extended the next invitation for a panel discussion on the Stanford campus. Dr. John Sallo, from San Francisco, Dr. Clara Fetter, from the Hoover Library, and Fr. Egon explained some aspects of the Russian communist oppression that led to the revolt. Fr. Egon spoke about the roles of youth, students, scholars, and writers. It drew a large audience and proved to be a long evening, because the time was not limited, and the students went on and on with questions into late hours. This occasion informed the Stanford people, through the presence of one Benedictine, that a private secondary school for boys would open soon next to their campus.

One result of the Hungarian revolt was unexpected. Receiving the news and hoping for the total liberation of Hungary, patriotism and nostalgia overwhelmed Fr. Christopher and Fr. Leopold. In special letters they announced to Fr. Brunner and to Fr. Egon their intention to return to Hungary as soon as possible and dedicate their lives to teaching the heroic youth of their native country. They made up their minds and wrote the letters under the influence of the early good news, when the future looked bright for Hungary. They cherished hopes, with wishful thinking, that the Benedictine Order would get back its schools and life would be normal for the Catholic Church, as before the communist takeover. Just at that time, Fr. Brunner issued a circular letter to all the fathers on November 3, before the Russians crushed the revolt. His message revealed a clear insight and solid objectivity in those turbulent times. Its content, abridged and translated from Hungarian, is as follows:

"The recent happenings in our mother-country implanted into the minds of all of us certain thoughts affecting our individual and community life. The future of Hungary as yet is uncertain. Even if it would turn for the better, the duration of it will remain questionable: how long will the Russians tolerate the break-away of one of their satellites? Let us not forget, our mother abbey wanted a foundation here in the United States. This intention has not been changed. We planned for seven years. This year we accepted a commitment in the Archdiocese of San Francisco, and we bought property for a monastery and school. We are obliged to stick to our decision and keep our commitments. Although our cause is small in comparison to the cause of the Hungarian nation and people, we have to continue to work and pray for our foundation in the United States."

The tragic end of the revolt made any hope for return impossible anyway. Deeply buried in their grief, the fathers prayed more for the poor oppressed people of Hungary and prepared with new zeal to meet in California.

It was impossible to seal the borders of Hungary immediately, so hundreds of thousands of refugees used the opportunity to flee the country and go to the West. The United States received with great generosity several thousand freedom fighters and their families. Fr. Egon was soon busy greeting his refugee compatriots at the airport, helping with translation and transportation, looking for lodging and work for the refugees, and even sharing the small ranch house with some of his former students or with relatives of his Hungarian Benedictine confreres. Among these were Father Charles Schilly and Father Pius Horvath, who in due time arrived in California and increased the number of the original seven. Bela Nemeth, later Fr. Maurus of the Priory, was 18 years old when he crossed the borders of his native land and, through the help of refugee organizations, found a new home in Canada. Several years later, while visiting in California, he discovered the Woodside Priory and his new vocation. He entered the order and studied for the priesthood. Thus the arrival of new Benedictines was a positive result of the revolt.

A great number of the freedom fighters and refugees were quite young, high school age. Most of them spoke only their native tongue. For the continuation of their educations, refugee organizations established Hungarian gymnasium schools in Austria and West Germany. These schools needed Hungarian teachers. For the location of one of the gymnasiums, the educational department of the German Republic offered the old building of Burg Kastl, a former Benedictine abbey in the Middle Ages. Fr. Gerard Bekes zealously advocated the acceptance of this place by the Hungarian Benedictines for their abbey and school in exile. The idea was not lacking in merit but came too late. The Hungarian fathers in Brazil, as well as in the United States, emphasizing their local commitments, declined the invitation to join. School was established in Burg Kastl, with some

Hungarian Benedictines teaching there, but never became exclusively a Benedictine abbey.

Fr. Egon soon experienced one other effect of the revolt in Hungary: donations went to the help of the refugees. Partly in admiration for their heroic efforts, partly for a feeling of guilt for not giving military help to that poor country, and a great deal from natural generosity, the Americans opened their pockets and poured their donations to the support of the freedom fighters. Fr. Egon received checks of small or large amounts with the request to direct them to the refugee organizations. When he asked for financial support for the Priory and revealed it to be a Hungarian foundation, he often got the friendly excuse: They just gave their donation to the Hungarian refugees. He also lost the pledges of the Hungarians whom he met in Los Angeles. Since almost every family supported either refugee relatives and friends or the more needy ones in the old country, it was understandable that they could not keep their promises. First comes first, the greater need must have precedence.

Fr. Egon remained confident that almighty God would show His Providence to the Priory in due time.

On November 10, 1956, Fr. Egon moved into the ranch house.

Chapter XIII

At Home—Again

It was on November 13, 1948, that Fr. Egon left his monastery and country. For seven years he was on the road, first as a stateless displaced person, later a refugee with some identification cards, and then an emigrant, living everywhere temporarily as a guest. Naturally he was looking forward to settling in a country, in a place, in a monastery that he could again call "home."

According to the agreement, Fr. Egon could take over their property in Portola Valley on November 1, but it was November 10 before he could move into their new home. The Gillsons, not well organized, had no one to help them. Mr. Harold Gillson and his wife came from the South, moved to California after their marriage, and bought the property with Mrs. Gillson's money. First they kept horses, and later Mr. Gillson became a traveling auto parts salesman and built racing cars with his own hands. Mrs. Gillson was often alone with her little daughter. She lived the life of a recluse, went nowhere, and did not associate with the neighbors. Mr. Gillson did the shopping and knew a few people around the stores and gasoline stations. They were not Catholic, had never met a priest in their lives, and kept a suspicious, cold distance from Fr. Egon.

The place looked quite neglected. The entrance road was not next to the Jelich property, as at present, but at the other side of the soccer field (between the existing two soccer fields), next to the Gambetta land. Two wagon wheels marked the entrance on Portola Road and on the big oak tree, a fading yellow and blue sign with the letter "G" informed the visitor that he had reached the Gillson ranch. Small acacia trees lined the side of the road leading in. The house was hardly visible from a distance: the palm tree, some pines, and old fruit trees (all quite small at the time) hid it fully. The picture was very rural and rustic; the rolling pastureland, which would be leveled for a soccer field, was divided with old wooden fences. The road led to the line of horse stables, their doors painted with the blue and yellow Gillson colors; to the left was a neglected corral, and to the right was the ranch house. One could drive up to the patio and reach the entrance door by climbing four or five stairs. Ivy framed the patio and the whole setting was attractive in its natural bucolic way.

Harold Gillson built everything himself, including his house. The walls were not parallel, the concrete floor undulated under one's steps, and the electrical switches were not correctly connected to the wiring. There was no central heating, but the large fireplace could warm the living room. The water heater and kitchen stove operated on butane that came in tanks every month. Except for the kitchen, the interior was not finished: cabinets, closets, and rooms lacked doors. One entered into the large living room. At the right end of this were two bedrooms with a bath between, to the left a small den, kitchen and utility room with washing equipment. The living room contained the dining area also. Icebox, stove, sink, and a redwood dining table with benches were included in the sale. There was no water service, but a well on the property, while not producing much water, supplied enough for the needs of a family of three.

Before moving in, Fr. Egon bought a good desk and some chairs at an auction and bought a new bed. A German cabinetmaker, Joseph Duller, from the Cupertino parish, made the altar according to given dimensions. On November 10, Mr. Joseph Pon took the flat truck from his fruit ranch and picked up Fr. Egon, the altar, desk, bed, and Fr. Egon's personal belongings, and they drove to Portola Valley. Mr. Pon helped with some cleaning and with carrying the furniture inside. The altar went into one bedroom making this the chapel; the desk and bed completed the other bedroom. The dining room area had the table, benches and two chairs. The first day passed quickly with the moving and cleaning. Around 5 o'clock, unexpected visitors, the De Potteres dropped in just for a few minutes, bringing salt and bread, according to an old European custom, to express their good wishes. St. Benedict wrote in his Rule: "Whatever good work you begin to do beg of Him (God) with most earnest prayers to perfect it." Following this admonition from the founder of his Order, Fr. Egon performed the prayerful ceremony of the old Roman "lucernarium" this evening. At sunset he changed into his best monastic habit. He took a blessed candle, preserved for this occasion, to the patio, lit it there, and walked into the house lifting the candle high and praying: Lumen Christi—as in the ceremony of the Easter Vigil. With the candle he lit the fire in the fireplace and blessed it. Then he walked around the house, blessed the rooms and the chapel equipment, and sprinkled holy water around. Afterward he relaxed before the fireplace and with a grateful heart blessed God for His wonderful work in leading him and his confreres out from the "servitude" of Hungary and giving them a new home in this "promised land" of California.

The next day, November 11, was the feast of St. Martin, the patron saint of the Abbey of Pannonhalma. Fr. Egon celebrated the first Mass on the Priory property according to the old Latin rites. The Medical Mission sisters loved the beauty of the liturgy and sang the Gregorian Mass with joyful devotion. About six of them drove over in a station wagon for this solemn occasion, having a hard time finding the place of the Benedictines. They brought the Mass equipment and left it as long as needed. They crowded into the small bedroom turned into the chapel and chanted the Gregorion melodies with heavenly beauty.

After the Mass they took over the kitchen and prepared a good breakfast, leaving pots and pans, dishes, and even food for Fr. Egon. For these young and hard working nuns the excursion meant more than a picnic; they were so happy with the rustic setting, walked all over the place, opened every door, looked into every room or stable, and enjoyed the day tremendously.

The following week some ladies from the Cupertino parish came over for a greatly needed cleaning of the whole building. They even dusted the walls, moved several lizard families into the open from the cabinets, and eliminated the spiders and cobwebs.

Fr. Egon discovered the second-hand stores on El Camino Real and bought some pieces of furniture; he also received many useful household items as donations.

The nuns who taught at the parish school in Cupertino loved to drive over, sometimes for Mass in the small chapel, sometimes for recreation. They never came empty handed and shared their food especially. They spread the word in the parish, now that they had their beautifully furnished, brand new convent, in what simplicity Fr. Egon lived. This brought other visitors with pieces of furniture or useful household equipment. Fr. Egon soon felt rich; some old carpets covered the concrete floor, curtains framed the windows, and the kitchen cabinets were well filled with provisions. At Christmas the ranch house looked quite good, equipped with one old radio, a second hand television set, and a vacuum cleaner–all Christmas gifts.

CHAPTER XIV

NEIGHBORS OF THE PRIORY

AFTER MOVING ONTO THE PROPERTY Fr. Egon paid his respects at the rectory of the local Catholic Church, Our Lady of the Wayside, and offered his services to the pastor. Fr. Guy Hayden needed help. On Sundays a priest drove out from St. Joseph's Seminary in Mountain View to assist him. He welcomed Fr. Egon and the services of the Benedictine fathers, who have faithfully served the parish since November 18, 1956. It was on that date that Fr. Egon celebrated Mass for the first time in Our Lady of the Wayside Church. Fr. Hayden announced the Benedictine school and priory after his Masses. Fr. Egon met some of the parishioners, including the Kielys who became very strong supporters of the Benedictines.

Soon other parishes and convents requested his priestly services. He often assisted Msgr. Kennedy at St. Raymond's. He also said Masses at the Convent of the Sacred Heart, at Vallombrosa retreat house in Menlo Park, and for the Holy Cross brothers at St. Francis High School. Fr. Egon often had dinner on Friday evenings at St. Francis High School.

On other days he said Mass at home, and to have some congregation around the altar, he used to invite families, neighbors, and friends. This worked well on Saturdays but not so well on weekdays. The closest neighbor, Mrs. Nunes from Georgia Lane, came most often, crossing the Breckenbridge orchard in the early mornings bringing flowers for the altar. She was Portuguese and could hardly understand Fr. Egon's English pronunciation. A retired colonel, Bob Dark, also dropped in often to offer his services.

However, as he was the daily server of Fr. Hayden and his most faithful helper at the parish church, Fr. Egon politely declined to accept his assistance.

Walter Jelich had his orchard next to the Priory but did not live there yet. He built his house and moved in during the summer of 1957.

On the other side of the Priory was the Gambetta ranch. Fr. Egon introduced himself to Mr. and Mrs. Gambetta. The Gillsons had boundary disputes with the Gambettas because of ditches, water drainage, fences, and transgressing animals, and they warned Fr. Egon that the Benedictines would be unwelcome neighbors. On the contrary, the Gambettas were friendly and hospitable to Fr. Egon. They lived the comfortable life of retired people. The dairy was closed by that time, the cows sold, and the barns empty. They told the story of their lives, the operation of the dairy with 200 cows, especially their long trip to Switzerland and Italy in 1947-48, and showed him many photographs. Fr. Egon met their son Louis, who lived next door, a big man of his own age. None of them expressed any opposition to the monastery or school. Although they were not practicing Catholics, they knew several priests and helped some religious causes in their birthplace, Italian Switzerland, demonstrating this with thank-you letters and brochures.

Not very far from the Priory on Portola Road stands the well-kept, elegant home of Norman and Emmy Davis. Mrs. Davis walked into the ranch house one morning when Fr. Egon was cleaning and introduced herself as a neighbor. Norman, her husband, held a high position as an engineer with United Airlines. Their only child, Kathleen, was about six years old. Norman and Emmy became most valuable friends and great helpers, not only of Fr. Egon, but also of the Priory and school. Mrs. Davis was a trained nurse and knew the society in the valley and on the Peninsula well. Fr. Egon could always trust her solid, sound judgment and good advice. Norman, extremely skilled in all works, extended his help whenever something needed repair around the house. He helped also in contacting persons or offices on business matters.

Mrs. Davis organized parties for ladies in her home, inviting mothers whose sons could become candidates for the Benedictine school, and she introduced Fr. Egon to many valuable families and promoted the Priory everywhere. She supplied Fr. Egon with many excellent dinners, bringing them over very modestly as "left over" from a party. They also included him in their family dinner at Thanksgiving.

The Davises organized a house warming party for Fr. Egon before Thanksgiving. Fr. Hayden and some families came, bringing useful gifts: a toaster, an iron with board, dishes, and glasses. All spent a friendly evening with coffee and cake in the living room. Some of those who were present are dead, some moved away, and some are still around: Admiral and Mrs. Quilter, the Boudreaus, the De Potteres, the Mirkos, Nichols, Garrasinos, and Skrabos, among others. Such events helped Fr. Egon to feel at home in Portola Valley.

Kathy Davis kept her first horse here in one of the stables and used the corral before her own was ready. She came daily to feed and exercise her lively horse. Other neighbors, Mr. and Mrs. Paul Randall, asked permission to use the large front pasture for a fine race horse for a few months. They operated the Union gas station on Portola Road at the Alpine corner. Through them Fr. Egon became acquainted over a period of time with the ranchers Jelich, Mariani, Duzanica, Skrabo, Volpiano, Jurian, Gomez, and Silveira in the neighborhood, and also with the younger cowboys and "horse people."

Chapter XV

Publicity

ON HIS TRIP TO LOS ANGELES, Fr. Egon learned the necessity of a good brochure with the name of the school and a fixed address.

In preparation for the brochure he consulted his colleagues concerning the name of the monastery and school. The selection of the name of the monastery was no problem. They all agreed easily on the name of King St. Stephen. The first king of Hungary invited the Benedictines into his country to bring the Christian religion and with it Western civilization to his people. By using the name of the first Hungarian saint in "King St. Stephen's Monastery," they assured the remembrance of this monastery's Hungarian origin. When all the Hungarian fathers are gone, and new generations of American monks pray in the chapel and teach in the school, the name of the monastery will remind visitors of its beginning: Hungarian Benedictines founded this monastery and school in California.

The selection of the name of the school was not so easy. Fr. Brunner was adamant in not naming the school after a saint, even after the most logical one, St. Benedict. Although this name might help to direct the mind toward the Order of St. Benedict and Benedictines, the average Americans, especially the Catholics, would associate the name with a parochial elementary or diocesan school, he thought. Breaking away from a saint's name, the name of the geographical location offered the most logical solution. This was the custom of other Benedictine schools: Portsmouth Priory and St. Louis

Priory. The actual location was in Portola Valley, but as yet there was not a town; it was only part of the county. The idea of Portola Priory came up, but the abbreviation could easily be abused by the youth of rival schools, calling the Priory students PP boys. They must be protected from such possible ridicule. Experience proved that not many people, even on the Peninsula, knew Portola Valley. The mail went on several occasions to Portola, a small town in northeastern California; even after mail service was established. Fr. Egon repeatedly had to answer inquiries about the location of the Priory. On the other hand, many people knew well where Woodside was: those who went to Stanford and many San Franciscans who owned summer places in Woodside and came to visit friends, attend horse shows, or picnic there. Consequently, the name Woodside Priory would indicate the geographical location of the school. Woodside was not an incorporated town at the time, either, but it was a good name and the fathers decided to use it.

Later, in November 1956, Woodside incorporated. The intention was to keep it small and rural, with about three or more acres as home sites. Just opposite the Priory, by an old county permit, houses were built on smaller lots. Woodside did not want this cheaper and more crowded area within its boundaries. Consequently this part of Portola Road and the Priory remained in the county, excluded by Woodside. In 1964, Portola Valley incorporated as a new community in California. Therefore, the Woodside Priory and Woodside Priory School are located in Portola Valley.

Mail service began in the valley in the spring of 1957. With the decision on a name for the school and a definite address, publicity was possible.

The credit goes to Mr. Richard P. Cooley for the preparation and the financing of the first brochure. He introduced Fr. Egon to Mr. Christopher E. Persons, a retired gentleman from the McCann & Ericson advertising firm in San Francisco, who was at that time an advisor to the public relations staff of Stanford University. He lived very close to the Priory in Los Altos and drove over often to visit Fr. Egon. They worked out the necessary materials during long discussions. Mr. Persons put together a good text with professional skill, emphasizing the importance of and the necessity for a new private school for boys on the Peninsula. Included was an accurate description of the Order of St. Benedict, its role in education for 14 centuries, and the backgrounds of the Hungarian fathers. The plans for the school were less clear, the details left vague. A map showed the location and gave the address. The need for financial support was moderately stressed. Through the intercession of Mr. Cooley, Mr. Charles Paganini, head of the Security Lithograph Company, offered to do the printing without charge. This first brochure was not only presentable, but quite attractive. On excellent paper, with fine printing, the text impressed readers. The cover illustration was a tall figure of a Benedictine monk lifting up the shield exhibiting the inscription "PAX." The brochure was ready for Christmas. Fr. Egon received plenty and distributed them generously. This brochure provided full scale publicity for three years.

Fr. Egon used all opportunities to appear before groups and present the Benedictine plans. The channels to invitations opened to him partly through the clergy and partly through his friendly supporters–Mr. Cooley, Mr. Cashin, and Mrs. Davis.

Mr. Cooley organized three or four luncheons at the Bohemian Club. Fr. Egon met with gentlemen of the business world in private rooms of downtown restaurants in the city. As a Benedictine alumnus, Mr. Cooley spoke about the Benedictine Order and their schools, then Fr. Egon spoke briefly and answered questions. The gentlemen whom he met at these occasions became, in one way or another, supporters of the Priory. Among them Joseph Alioto, Atherton Phleger, Marshall Madison, and Robert Miller were lawyers; Fernand Stent, Michael Tobin, and Donald Lahey were bankers; and Charles Harney, Paul Fay, Jr., and John Cahill were contractors. Some evening receptions took place in private homes in the city where friends or neighbors of the host gathered before dinner. Fr. Egon met large groups of prominent Catholics in the homes of the Cooleys and the Eidells.

The Eidells were a prominent family in San Francisco. He was a successful investment banker, and she was very active in social circles. Being friends of the Cooleys, they organized a highly successful party with thirty guests at their home on Broadway. Fr. Egon was able to present the Benedictines, describe their education, and answer questions.

Another dinner took place through the efforts of Emmet Cashin in the Hillsborough home of Mr. Moore, whose married daughters became quite active in promoting the Priory around San Mateo and Burlingame. Emmet Cashin brought Fr. Egon together with a young lawyer, Howard Daschbach, of Atherton. Through him, Fr. Egon addressed the Palo Alto group of the Serra Club at their regular meeting in Palo Alto. They met in a large private dining room at Rickey's with about 50 or 60 professional men from the vicinity. Many of the sons of those present became students in the early years of the Woodside Priory School. After this occasion, the Serrans asked Fr. Egon to speak in San Jose and in other towns as far away as Stockton. He was also invited by the Crespi Club to address a group of retired professional gentlemen in Atherton at a luncheon.

Mrs. Norman Davis promoted the Benedictines among the ladies. Through her efforts Fr. Egon spoke to the mothers at the girls schools: Sacred Heart School in Menlo Park and at Notre Dame in Belmont. Many of these mothers had also expressed interest in a private school for their sons. Mrs. Davis gave several parties for ladies in her own home and through her prompting Fr. Egon was invited to speak to mothers in some homes in Atherton and Menlo Park.

The Ray Folger family gave a fine dinner and gathered many of their friends in the evening to meet the Benedictine father. Again, many of those present became generous supporters of the Priory or sent their sons to the Benedictine school. It was in this way that Fr. Egon met the Flippens, the Wynnes, the Lussiers, and others.

Mrs. John Kiely told the Robert F. Gill family of Woodside of the arrival of the Benedictines in the valley. They invited Fr. Egon for dinner and soon became good friends and very generous supporters of the new school. They not only introduced Fr. Egon to their relatives and to many of their friends in Woodside, but also organized several parties in their home, giving Fr. Egon the opportunity to meet people and to answer questions. Through their efforts, the local Woodsiders became acquainted with the Woodside Priory and school.

In 1958 neighbors were selling five acres on the hill adjacent to the Priory land. When Fr. Egon mentioned this to the Gills, they told him to get a loan to buy the land, and they would donate the sum in five year installments. With the help of Mr. Cooley, the Madison Foundation proceeded with the loan, and by the generosity of the Gills the Priory property grew to 23 acres.

Another means of publicity was through parishes. Interested pastors, especially those whose parishes operated elementary schools, invited Fr. Egon to speak to parent groups, members of Holy Name societies, or other guilds. Although this was a good method of making the Order of St. Benedict and the presence of the Benedictine fathers on the Peninsula better known, from the point of view of the school, it ran into difficulty. Where the Catholic high school for boys was close to the parish, as Serra, Bellarmine, and St. Francis, recruiting looked impolite or impractical, except for the very few who sought a boarding school. The question of tuition always came from the parents with the subject of private schools. It became painful to say frankly that it would be expensive, according to the condition laid down by Archbishop Mitty; otherwise the school would lure students from the established Catholic high schools. Many good parents, who very much wanted a good education for their children but could not afford it, were saddened by this answer. Fr. Egon had to discern carefully to which group he could emphasize the Benedictine Order and to which the Benedictine education and school.

The press and television started to show interest toward the end of the spring when construction began, and a benefit fashion show was in preparation for the Priory school. The efforts of ladies, especially of Mrs. Norman Davis, brought photographers and reporters to the Priory grounds, and pictures and articles appeared in the local papers announcing the opening of a new college preparatory school for boys in Portola Valley.

Fr. Egon got an appointment with Mr. Charles Thieriot, the editor of the San Francisco Chronicle, with the help of Mrs. Cameron, whose family owned the paper. Mr. Thieriot had been a Benedictine student at the Portsmouth Priory in the very early days of the school when the fathers and the lay masters were still very demanding in academics and very strict in discipline. He did not have good recollections of his connections with the Benedictines and made it frankly clear to Fr. Egon. However, he was gracious enough to forward the cause of the Hungarian Benedictines (the memory of the revolt made Hungarian topics still newsworthy in the spring of 1957) and placed Fr. Egon in the hands of a reporter. Consequently a good article brought the news to the attention of the readers of the San Francisco Chronicle.

Promotions of the fashion show at the home of Mrs. Ralph K. Davies appeared on two different television programs. The first one was one weekday morning. Fr. Egon escorted Mrs. Marshall P. Madison to the television station and both answered certain questions, Mrs. Madison concerning the fashion show, and Fr. Egon concerning the Benedictines and their school. The other took place one Sunday afternoon. Mrs. Norman Davis came along, but Fr. Egon was alone on the program that lasted only a few minutes.

The first buildings, the monastery (right) and a classroom, were built in 1957.

CHAPTER XVI

FIRST BUILDING

WHEN FR. EGON LEFT THE PARISH IN CUPERTINO he found himself without an income. Moving into their new home filled him with joy, but also with the burden of paying monthly bills. All of his savings, and the savings of all the other Hungarian fathers, went into the down payment for the property. Up to now, living in monasteries and in the parish, he was provided with room and board. Now, for the first time in his life in the United States, he had to pay for his daily food, for phone and electricity, for butane gas, for insurance and service on the car, and for insurance on the ranch house. All of these he could cover with the modest sums he got for helping in parishes and occasionally for his talks and retreats. In early February, when a bill of over $700 came for the taxes on the property, he was shocked and did not know where to turn for the money. The property was not tax exempt as the school had not opened. Then, just before the payment was due, he received a letter from Mr. Leo Fisher, a Hungarian industrialist whom he met in Los Angeles the previous October. Mr. Fisher sent a donation with an apology, explaining that the larger part of his generosity must go to help the refugee Hungarian Freedom Fighters who had arrived in great numbers in Los Angeles. However, he wished to help the Benedictine fathers with a small gift. He sent a check for $800; Fr. Egon could pay the property tax without delay.

This was the first tangible gesture of Divine Providence that the fathers experienced continually during the hard early years of the Priory. From somebody, from somewhere, the necessary amount always arrived, through the abundance of Divine Providence; so much so that the fathers were never delinquent in paying their important bills or loans on time. It became a proverb on their lips, "Almighty God helps as always, sometimes only in the 25th hour." The same gesture of Divine Providence assisted Fr. Egon when the question of construction arose.

One day toward the end of February, Mrs. Norman Davis came with her daughter to the Priory grounds to feed their horse. In a long conversation with Fr. Egon she seriously warned him about his imminent duties. If the Benedictines really planned to open a school here in September, there was no time to lose in selecting the architect, preparing the master plan and beginning the first construction. Fr. Egon had to admit openly that his group simply had no money to hire an architect or to pay for buildings. All that they had was absorbed in the down payment for the property.

Mrs. Davis was aghast, but made good use of this bad news. A few days later Mr. John Kiely came to visit Fr. Egon. He brought his donation, a check for $2,000 and his pledge that he would enroll his second son in this new school. He would then donate the same amount, in addition to tuition fees, until the graduation of Michael Kiely. Many other gifts followed, mostly as the result of introductions and the publicity previously mentioned. Some were in the amount of $1,000 or even more. Mrs. Emmy Davis continued her helpful activity. One day she offered the idea of a fashion show for the benefit of the Priory. This, if well organized, would bring publicity and cash.

At the urging of Fr. Egon, Fr. Brunner mailed letters to some of the well-established American Benedictine abbeys. He informed them of the plans of the Hungarian monks and asked for loans. Two abbots responded with positive help: St. Vincent Archabbey in Pennsylvania and St. John's Abbey in Minnesota, each offering $5,000 in loans for ten years. By correspondence one other $10,000 loan was secured through Fr. Gerard Bekes, who had some money of the Hungarian Benedictines in trust in Rome and could send part of it for a few years.

In early March, Fr. Egon visited Mr. Cooley, informing him of the improved financial situation. Through his intervention the Hibernia Bank was willing to advance a loan also. All of these gifts and loans made the construction of the first building possible.

Mr. Cooley directed Fr. Egon to Mr. John Cahill for the selection of an architect. Since Fr. Egon had visited many schools on the Peninsula, he had developed some conceptions of the buildings he wanted for the Priory, and he had the names of those architects whose buildings he liked best. Mr. Cahill eliminated the idea of a master plan immediately with the sober comment that it was not yet necessary and there was no money for it. He did not accept the name of any architect offered by Fr. Egon because they designed buildings that were too expensive. He recommended a modest firm and took Fr. Egon to the office of Mr. Bolton White, on Green Street in San Francisco.

Without a master plan, the work of the architect was easy. Mr. Cahill instructed him to save in every way possible. Consequently, the first monastery building was not large: eleven rooms for the monks, one small reception room, and a large community reading room, which at first served as the chapel. The building sat close to the existing ranch house on a higher elevation on the hillside. Mr. Cahill wanted to make the rooms smaller, telling Fr. Egon that the master bedroom in his own home was only a bit larger and two shared it; why should the monks have such large bedrooms? Fr. Egon had to defend the size of the rooms vigorously. For a monk the room served not only as a bedroom, but also as office and his only place of privacy, where all of his intellectual work was done. As the monks did their own cleaning, a room too small could never be kept in order; he knew that from the experience of seeing many monasteries. His firmness proved to be beneficial in the future. When the monastic community grew, several of these rooms became two small bedrooms in the 1960's.

The blueprints were drawn and bids came in and were considered. A small and inexpensive contractor, Mr. George Dugan, was ready to start the construction without delay. It was in the middle of May when he, while inspecting the building site, surprised Fr. Egon with the question of when would the excavation of the site be done and by whom? This was a shock to Fr. Egon. He thought the contractor's bid included the entire job. Time was pressing and a company willing to do the necessary excavation must be found immediately. He visited several contractors in the vicinity;

all were too busy with more important and more lucrative jobs. Only L.C. Smith from San Mateo sent out an estimator. He not only disappointed Fr. Egon by telling him that his firm could not start the work for a few weeks, but that it would cost over $6,000. Fr. Egon did not know how to hurdle this unexpected obstacle. The fathers would arrive soon after the end of the school year; the monastery must be ready.

While he was absorbed in this problem, visitors arrived one Sunday afternoon. During his stay in Cupertino, he gave instruction in the Catholic religion to one of the parishioners, who embraced the faith and who Fr. Egon baptized. This gentleman, Roger McElligot, drove in with his family. While inspecting the property and walking on the hillside, Fr. Egon mentioned his problem concerning the excavation. His guest said, "Why don't you go to Tony Voss?" also a member of the St. Joseph parish in Cupertino, a good Catholic and owner of a large road construction company.

Following this advice, Fr. Egon turned to Mr. Voss, explaining to him both the urgency of and the lack of money for the work, very frankly. Mr. Voss knew Fr. Egon from the parish and was most sympathetic with the problem of the Benedictine fathers. He recalled that he started his business with one small truck and even borrowed money to buy it. Now he owned hundreds of large and expensive pieces of equipment and was just about to retire, selling his business to the Sondgrath Brothers. He drove out to inspect the place the same day. He promised to start the work and in payment asked just a small reward. One of his sisters was a nun in the Order of Notre Dame de Namur. She studied chemistry at some university and just recently had broken an instrument in the laboratory. Mr. Voss charged the Benedictine fathers to pay for this instrument. Fr. Egon happily accepted the deal and mailed the sum (about $300) to Sister Voss.

The next day and for the following two weeks, the roar of a big bulldozer enchanted the heart of Fr. Egon. Mr. Voss estimated the work would take one week, but without the help of a carrier, the machine had to push the dirt from the cut farther and farther away on the fill, and so it took longer. Fr. Egon also used the presence of the equipment to bring dirt to fill space at the side and front of the ranch house and make it look more attractive. Later, during the construction of the monastery, the addition of a concrete patio and walkway assured a good-looking entrance to this rustic country house.

Soon they poured the foundation, and the frame of the monastery building became visible on the hillside. New photographs were made for publicity with two "first" students, Michael Kiely and Dick Pierce, watching the construction.

Fr. Egon continued doing spiritual work, preaching a retreat to the alumni of the Sacred Heart Schools in Menlo Park and a day of recollection to the mothers of the students of Notre Dame High School in Belmont. After this, he could turn his full attention to the preparation of the fashion show for the benefit of the Priory.

When Mrs. Norman Davis suggested a benefit fashion show, Fr. Egon accepted it with gratitude, without having the faintest idea of what a tremendous amount of work was involved. He learned a lot following the preparations step by step, especially to admire and appreciate the working ability and efficiency of American women. He participated in many meetings and had his share in the physical preparation also.

On Mrs. Davis' advice, Fr. Egon asked Mrs. Kiely to be the chairwoman of this event, and she graciously accepted. When the friends from Hillsborough learned of a fashion show for the Priory, they joined in. Mrs. Marian McGuire Moore offered her services and became the co-chairwoman. Mrs. Ralph Davies and Mrs. Marshall Madison were invited to be honorary chairwomen and the former kindly opened her beautiful estate in Woodside for the location of the benefit. Through their connections the ladies got the Elizabeth Arden firm to present their fashions.

Selection of the date caused some problems because of graduations and parties at the end of the school year. Also there was the possibility of a late rain. Finally, they selected June 5. The publicity was extensive and varied. Luncheon parties were given in different homes in the area. Photographers took pictures in the home of the Kielys and in the gardens of Mrs. Ralph Davies. Ladies on horseback appeared on the Priory property to have pictures taken for fashion show promotion. Posters appeared in busy store entrances, and articles advertised it in the papers. Mrs. Madison with Fr. Egon, also

Mrs. Davies and Mrs. McBain, were on television and radio, speaking about the benefit show for the new Benedictine school. Attractive programs contained photographs.

June 5 was a splendid day. The weather was sunny. It was not too hot, just perfect for the fashion show. Nine hundred chairs were set up in the garden of the Davies estate and fresh flowers in large vases decorated the entrance. The advance sales of tickets indicated a large attendance. Publicity attracted people: many came to see the newest fashions, others to enjoy the beauty of Mrs. Ralph Davies' house and gardens, others to help the Priory. The nine hundred seats were soon taken, and chairs had to be carried out from the house.

Mrs. Davies, quite exhausted, had no seat for herself and watched the show seated on the edge of the planters. Mrs. Madison welcomed the guests. Fr. Egon then thanked all for their support with a few words combining the beauty of the setting with the worthy goal of the benefit. The financial success was good, far above expectations. Mrs. Norman Davis had the lion's share of the work, and consequently, the joy of the success.

Some of those present drove over after the fashion show to the Priory grounds to see the location. The day ended by cleaning up at Mrs. Davies' house, and a good group of the workers gathered for a closing celebration party and dinner at the home of the Kielys, where Fr. Egon accepted the proceeds of the day in a check and expressed his gratitude for this benefit fashion show.

During these days the welcome noise of construction–roar of trucks, bang of hammering, and smell of tar–filled the Priory grounds and vicinity. Walter Jelich's house, next door, was also under construction at that time. A few days after the fashion show an unexpected late rain arrived. Torrents of water fell on the grounds during the night. It was welcome, as they needed rain. The rushing water washed off the new fill from the building elevation and the rear end of the ranch house became partly buried by mud. It took days for Fr. Egon to excavate it and free access to the back door of the ranch house. The entrance road was also inundated and only by using wooden boards and stepping-stones was it possible to reach the main entrance door from the car for a few days.

Fr. Leopold (right) took over the supervision of the construction from Fr. Egon after his arrival in June, 1957.

Chapter XVII

The Community Comes Together at Woodside Priory

At the end of the school year in 1957, the Hungarian fathers finished their work and obligations where they were and were free to move to California.

Fr. Emod Brunner and Fr. Leopold Hoffer started first, deciding to drive across the continent. Fr. Leopold traded in the car he had for a new Chevrolet station wagon. This would have room for them and their belongings and then be used at the school. Fr. Leopold drove from Jesuit University in Baltimore to New York to pick up Fr. Brunner. They left on June 23 and expected to arrive in early July. They took the Southern route, planning to visit some interesting places, but they stopped only at the Grand Canyon. They suffered from the heat and could not sleep well in motels, so Father Leopold drove fast, eager to arrive soon. Fr. Emod had not yet learned to drive so the job fell to Fr. Leopold.

On June 27, Fr. Egon was in the midst of a great cleaning when he got a phone call from Fr. Leopold that they were in Bakersfield. They would arrive that afternoon. The two drove in around 3:00 p.m., tired and sleepy, wanting to have a good shower and quiet rest. Just then, when Fr. Egon was so eager to have everything in good order for their arrival, their early appearance became a disaster: the house was without water.

A small well supplied the ranch house with water when Fr. Egon moved in. This well was enough for the use of a family of three. The seller did not mention that occasionally it did not satisfy their needs. In May, to improve the entrance to the house, dirt from the excavation from the monastery site was moved in front of the house and grass was planted for the lawn. This needed regular irrigation that slowly exhausted the water supply. Not only did the grass not grow well, but there was no water in the building either. This was a sad welcome for the first arrivals. Luckily the monastery building needed city water, the pipes were already underground, and the problem was solved the next day. In spite of this incident, their reunion was happy. Cold drinks and some Friday supper were ready. There were beds: the one for Fr. Brunner was in a small laundry room, and Fr. Leopold slept on the couch of the living room. The next day they inspected the property and the monastery. The construction was approaching completion. Neither gas, nor electricity nor even the water was connected when Fr. Stanley flew in from New York one week after the two early arrivals. Painting was in progress, but windows and doors were still missing. To prepare lodging for all, Fr. Leopold and Fr. Egon moved out the chapel equipment and the altar.

Fr. Christopher visited relatives in Michigan then joined Fr. Benignus in Newark, N.J. They drove across the continent and arrived on August 15, 1957.

Fr. Achilles flew in for a few weeks as a visitor. His original agreement with St. John's Abbey in Minnesota kept him there for one more year. He intended to stay at St. John's for good and teach theology instead of teaching in a high school. Only when the good fathers there convinced him that his place was with those in Portola Valley and that he could do more service in the newborn monastery did he come to stay in the summer of 1958.

As of August 15, 1957, all the fathers were at home in the monastery. This building had ten rooms for the monks. The chapel was to the right of the monastery entrance; opposite was a smaller multipurpose room: office or parlor for visitors, guest room or sick room in case of need (it had a bathroom). The next room was a bit larger for the superior. After the separate chapel was built, that room became the community recreation room and library as planned. The other rooms were all the same size, equipped with desk, chairs, bed, washing basin, medicine cabinet, closet, and curtains. The furniture was first borrowed from friends and later bought in second hand stores on El Camino or at auction. Only the bedding was bought new. In the middle of the building were the showers and lavatories, a phone booth, and a utility room.

After the long years of dispersion and of individual lifestyle the community life began. Frs. Emod, Egon, and Stanley worked out the order of the day and the principal rules for the monastic discipline. (There was no concelebration before Vatican II.)

The fathers said individual Masses. The full choir was established, still in Latin, using the Breviarium Maurinum of the Hungarian Congregation. For their habits, they continued to wear the habit of the American Cassinese Congregation (not that of Pannonhalma), which became obligatory in chapel, classes, meals, and at all official events. Fr. Emod was not appointed or voted to be prior and did not want the title. He called himself superior and headmaster. It was his wish that his substitute be elected. Fr. Christopher, senior next to Fr. Emod, received two votes, Fr. Egon, three, so he became the substitute for the superior. Fr. Leopold was appointed to do the maintenance and held the title of procurator. Fr. Stanley became the treasurer.

Although those who had just arrived wanted to discover California or at least the vicinity of the Priory, they had hard work to do for the opening of the school year. Fr. Egon gave them the necessary background and prepared Fr. Emod with everything he needed to know as superior. The two of them worked on the finances and loans for the school building. Fr. Leopold took over the supervision of construction. Frs. Leopold, Christopher, and Stanley worked on the curriculum, books, school calendar, etc. All were involved in deciding the character of the school. For the sake of a good education they decided to teach on Saturdays.

They realized that without funds and buildings they could not open a boarding school. However, they accepted resident students. The ranch house contained the kitchen and dining room. The two bedrooms with the bathroom between them were converted and equipped for six resident students. Fr. Egon became their housemaster and moved into the remaining room.

The acceptance of boarding students brought the solution to the problem of cooking. When the fathers came together this question came up: who will take over the kitchen and the cooking?

They could not afford to hire a person for this job. None of the group could cook or was willing to volunteer. Finally Fr. Emod exercised not only his authority but also his humor. He said, "Fr. Leopold has a doctorate in biology; he knows what is poisonous and what is edible. Let him take care of the kitchen." According to the old Latin proverb, "monachus ad omnia aptus," the monk is able for any task. Fr. Leopold took this remark seriously; he was in the kitchen the next morning and started to cook for the community. In one week he gained six pounds. This convinced the others that whatever he served was not only edible, but nourishing. Fr. Leopold cooked for the rest of the summer, and later on weekends or holidays when there was no outside help. He learned to love cooking. With the income from the boarding students the fathers were soon able to hire a lady cook, who served them and the boarding students Monday through Friday.

The seven exiled refugee Hungarian Benedictine monks settled happily in their new home in Portola Valley, California, and opened their college preparatory school in September 1957.

Their hearts were full of gratitude and joy. They thanked in fervent prayer the goodness of Almighty God, who guided their footsteps from Russian occupied communist Hungary into the hospitable shores of the United States where they could continue their monastic life renewing the Benedictine motto "Ora et Labora;" they prayed and worked at Woodside Priory.